Praise for S

"*Sister Roar* is a beautiful book. A gift for our time! Miss Kay and Lisa share their stories in a way that invites women to seek the healing and strength that come from healthy female community and to believe in the hope that each woman has an irreplaceable life, story, and mission. Most of all, they encourage women to live the fullest of lives by surrendering to and embracing their best friend and Savior—Jesus—who makes mercy, joy, mission, and healing possible."

—Jeanne Mancini, president of March for Life

"Sisterhood is sacred for me. I lost both my sisters at an early age. My big sister, Charlotta, was killed in a car accident when she was twenty. My little sister, Cheralyn, died a few years later from leukemia when she was fifteen. By the time I was eighteen, I was very aware of a missing connection in my life: sisters. Finding that inner circle of sisters took years for me. This book will enhance the process for you. You will find your circle. Your tribe. Your sisterhood! You will grow together. Trust life and God together. Change your world together. And, yes, our sisterhood will even *roar* together."

—Chonda Pierce, comedian and author

"It is such an honor and privilege to endorse this amazing book *Sister Roar*, coauthored by Lisa Robertson and her mother-in-law Miss Kay. I know that every word in this powerful book is true, because I have been privileged to call these two amazing women my friends. This is one of the most impactful books I have ever read to help the broken and downtrodden receive healing and find their voice to help others."

—Nancy Alcorn, founder and president of Mercy Multiplied

"I am inspired by the real and raw faith of Lisa and Miss Kay. This book digs deeply into the struggles women are facing, and then points us to the cross and the power and purpose of our identity in Christ. Grateful for their wisdom and writings here."

—Megan Alexander, TV host and author of *Faith in the Spotlight*

"*Sister Roar* is a powerful book. It makes you laugh, cry, smile, wince, and blush. But at the end, you will feel energized with the power that comes from the divinely inspired sisterhood of Lisa, Miss Kay, and their cast of characters. They point the way to the true and only source of power: Jesus Christ. And they teach us to use our voices to roar one another on to victory in our own circles. This book would be impactful to read alone, in a small group, or in a large ministry. I can't wait to see how the Lord uses this book for such a time as this."

—Pam Pryor, former State Department acting assistant secretary for International Organization Affairs and faith outreach director for the 2016 presidential campaign

"Every human has experienced some sort of difficulty in their lifetime. And if you are a woman, you more than likely desire to have another woman in your life you can talk to and share your feelings with. As a Christian, I know that the Scripture says, 'For where two or three gather in my name, there am I with them' (Matthew 18:20). It brings me comfort to know that when I gather with my sisters in Christ, our Lord is there with us—hearing our pain, sorrow, sadness, and joy. Together, we can make our requests known to Him who has the power to heal, restore, and redeem. Knowing this makes life sweeter and hard times easier to bear, and it gives us the strength to find our voice when we want to give in to the temptation to isolate ourselves. You will get encouragement in *Sister Roar* to find space where you can grow in your faith and your roar that is just waiting to be heard."

—Jackie Green, author and cofounder of the Museum of the Bible

Sister
ROAR

Sister ROAR

Claim Your Authentic Voice, Embrace Real Freedom, and Discover True Sisterhood

Kay Robertson + Lisa Robertson

WITH AMI McCONNELL

An Imprint of Thomas Nelson

Sister Roar

Published in Nashville, Tennessee, by Nelson Books, an imprint of Thomas Nelson. Nelson Books and Thomas Nelson are registered trademarks of HarperCollins Christian Publishing, Inc.

Published in association with Yates & Yates, www.yates2.com.

Thomas Nelson titles may be purchased in bulk for educational, business, fundraising, or sales promotional use. For information, please e-mail SpecialMarkets@ThomasNelson.com.

ISBN: 978-1-4002-3549-0 (Audiobook)
ISBN: 978-1-4002-3561-2 (TP))

Library of Congress Cataloging-in-Publication Data

Names: Robertson, Kay, 1947- author. | Robertson, Lisa, 1966- author.
Title: Sister roar : claim your authentic voice, embrace real freedom, and discover true sisterhood / Kay Robertson and Lisa Robertson.
Description: Nashville, Tennessee : Nelson Books, [2022] | Summary: "In Sister Roar, Duck Dynasty matriarch Miss Kay and her daughter-in-law Lisa empower their sisters in faith to discover their true voices, build genuine sisterhood, and live their strongest, happiest, most fulfilled lives--all centered around the only One who loves perfectly--Jesus"--Provided by publisher.
Identifiers: LCCN 2021050532 (print) | LCCN 2021050533 (ebook) | ISBN 9781400235452 (hardcover) | ISBN 9781400235469 (ebook)
Subjects: LCSH: Christian women--Religious life. | Sisters--Religious life. | Christian life.
Classification: LCC BV4527 .R5835 2022 (print) | LCC BV4527 (ebook) | DDC 248.8/43--dc23/eng/20211208
LC record available at https://lccn.loc.gov/2021050532
LC ebook record available at https://lccn.loc.gov/2021050533

Printed in the United States of America

23 24 25 26 27 LBC 5 4 3 2 1

To all the women who read this book and say, "Hey, that's me! I struggle with that, I've done that, and, Satan, I'm done with your lies! I'm worthy, I'm forgiven, and Christ loved me so much that He gave his life for me! I'll sing His praises and ignore your lying whispers."

We lift each one of you up to the Father!
We pray God's sweet blessing on you and
all with whom you share this book!

Contents

Foreword

Growing up I got to see a lot of strong women. I was surrounded by women who knew the Lord and spoke boldly about Him. They were not afraid to tell you about the gospel, fry a fish, or even cook a squirrel! These women helped shape me into the speaker, sister, friend, and mom I am today. They are the ones who showed me the way.

Two of these women are the very ones for whose book I am writing the foreword at this moment. If you ever watched *Duck Dynasty*, you no doubt know Miss Kay and Lisa, or Mamaw Kay and Aunt Lisa to me. They were sure to be found in the kitchen making a delicious meal out of whatever their husbands had just shot or caught. But, more importantly, you no doubt know their voices. They never failed to ring out the truth about the love of Jesus to someone during the episode.

As I stepped into the spotlight, I had moments when I didn't know how to use my voice. It felt like everyone was watching me and expecting something different from me. I had moments when I felt like I needed to conform to who the world wanted me to be. But then I would look around at the examples I had in my life, like Aunt Lisa and Mamaw Kay, who didn't conform to the world and were living out the life Christ had for them. And I knew that was what I truly desired over fame.

They showed me that we are not in this world to please man, but to please only Him (Galatians 1:10). They showed me the value in using my voice and words to change the lives of others.

Growing up I also got to hear their stories of pain, loss, and forgiveness. Their own hard life experiences gave me the wisdom to deal with the hard times in my life. They gave me the freedom to know that I don't have to be perfect to be used by God; I just have to be willing and faithful. They taught me the power of prayer, and how He answers even in the silent moments (1 John 5:14). They taught me the value of community, leaning on those God places in your life so that the tough moments are a little bit easier (Hebrews 10:25).

I know when you read their stories, you will get to see that it was not their own strength that got them through the craziness of their lives but their reliance on the strength and love of Christ. Even in tough times, their strength is the joy of the Lord. I can hear their laughter in my ears right now as I think about how much fun they managed to have in a world that can be hard to live in.

And through it all, they did it together—as sisters. They leaned on each other, gave each other advice, and told each other the truth through Scripture. Seeing this changed the way I relate to others, knowing that every sister of mine matters and has a voice that God gave her to use. The tag line of my ministry Live Original is: "be a good sister and friend." This book will teach you how.

From reading this book, I hope you will experience a little

bit of the life-giving advice my aunt and grandma gave me. From reading their words, I hope will you get to see how they experienced Christ throughout their lives, how it changed them, and how they then used it to change the lives of others.

My ministry, my voice, and my message would not be in the place they are now without the voice—without the *roar*—of these women. The impact their stories have had on my life allows me to tell mine without fear, because I know the value of God's redemptive nature through healing and sharing.

I pray that you will experience the goodness of God through them, just as I have.

Sadie Robertson Huff
December 8, 2021

Introduction

Hello, Sister!

I pray that the eyes of your heart may be enlightened in order that you may know the hope to which he has called you, the riches of his glorious inheritance in his holy people.

EPHESIANS 1:18

Ever heard of a hunter named Phil Robertson?

This fella crafted a duck call years and years ago. This was no ordinary duck call. And Phil was no ordinary hunter. When other hunters discovered how good Phil's Duck Commander call was, they loved it. He had to make a lot more! With the help of his wife, Kay, and their sons, Alan, Willie, Jase, and Jep, the Robertson family business was born. They made duck hunting videos and decoys too. After a lot of trial and error and decades of hard work, they'd built a multimillion-dollar hunting empire.

That's when producers from A&E Network came calling. They figured those tough, burly Robertson men with their unruly beards and their funny, close-knit, small-town Louisiana family might make a good reality television series. So they filmed a couple of pilots and *Duck Dynasty* was born. It became the number one reality TV show in America, running for five years. It's still airing today and holds the title of highest-rated reality TV show. That's how Phil and his faithful, fun-loving family became celebrities known the world over.

So that brings you up to date. Now let us introduce ourselves.

Miss Kay is the Robertson family matriarch—wife of Phil and backbone-slash-funny-bone of the family. You might have seen her on television, eaten at one of her restaurants, or drooled your way through one of her *New York Times* best-selling cookbooks.

And I'm Lisa. I'm Kay's daughter-in-law. I am married to Alan, the "beardless brother" (though, truth be told, he sports a short one these days).

Unlike our husbands, Miss Kay and I do not hunt or fish. The boys catch 'em and we cook 'em. We might be physically unintimidating, but we are fierce in our own way. By God's grace, Kay and I have been kin by marriage in this incredible family for more than thirty years. We're independent and strong, but we're even better together.

We're big on hospitality where we come from, so right off, we'd like to welcome you in and call you "sister."

That's right. We're calling you sister because when you love somebody, you call them by name and sometimes by terms of endearment. The way we figure it, women all over the world are our sisters because of our genetic makeup. But there's a profound sense in which Christian women truly are family. Thanks to Jesus' great sacrifice on the cross, God calls each of us his own daughter. So in this book, we hope you'll see yourself as our sister, and we are truly grateful you've chosen to spend some time with us in the following pages.

Now that you understand the *Sister* part of the title, let us explain what we mean by the term *Roar*. Imagine for a moment a big ole cat. Let's say a lioness—a truly majestic animal. Lions are animal royalty. Can't you just see those piercing eyes and razor-sharp teeth? That lithe body, coiled and ready to pounce? Like another bearded family you might know (hint, hint), lions live together in groups called prides.

One lion is fierce. A pride? Invincible.

A lion's roar is impossible to imitate, even for Phil!

All big cats roar—lions, tigers, leopards, jaguars, lynx, and cheetahs. It's a sound that can intimidate rivals, warn other cats of danger, or simply say, "I'm here!" A feline roar can be heard from as far as five miles away. Think about it this way: it's twenty-five times louder than a gas-powered lawn mower.[1]

Simply put, a roar is powerful.

That kind of raw power is inside of you, sister. You are a daughter of the King. You're not animal royalty; you're divine royalty! That's your identity.

> You are God's chosen and special people. You are a group of royal priests and a holy nation. God has brought you out of darkness into his marvelous light. Now you must tell all the wonderful things that he has done. The Scriptures say,
>
> "Once you were nobody.
> Now you are God's people.
> At one time no one
> had pity on you.
> Now God has treated you
> with kindness."
>
> (1 Peter 2:9–10 CEV)

Jesus, God's Son, gave up everything so that we can also be called heirs. He's the Lion of Judah.

> See, the Lion of the tribe of Judah, the Root of David, has triumphed. He is able to open the scroll and its seven seals. (Revelation 5:5)

And he's our brother!

The experiences you've had, the decisions you've made, the talents you possess, the dreams you hold in your heart, your quirkiest quirks—they're all part of what makes you special. You are God's masterpiece.

> You made all the delicate, inner parts of my body
> and knit me together in my mother's womb.
> Thank you for making me so wonderfully
> complex!
> Your workmanship is marvelous—how well I
> know it. (Psalm 139:13–14 NLT)

Just as every lion has a special roar, each of us has a unique sound. It's how the world knows who you are and what matters to you. It's a thing of beauty. It's the distinct way you express the person you were created to be. It's an expression of life, hope, and God-given purpose. It attracts; it doesn't repel. It's your way of living the life you're created for, making a difference in the lives of those around you.

When others hear your roar, they instinctively respond.

Maybe you haven't given much thought to your unique

sound. Even so, it's inside of you. It might whisper. It might sing. It might rush up and flow out of you like a praise song. Like a lion in a pride, a woman's strength is multiplied in good company. Surrounded by true, godly friends, she's stronger. Safer from threats and danger. And ready to take on the world. A roar is a sound other women will respond to. They respond when they feel the strength God put within you when he knit you in your mother's womb and nurtured you throughout your life.

At certain times in your life, your roar might have gone completely quiet. It might have been snuffed out or put on hold. Maybe you've longed to voice it, but something or someone denied you that permission. That opportunity. Maybe that "something" is a regret or a mistake. Maybe it's a real or perceived weakness. It could be a pain, a trauma so deep that forgiving the person who caused it seems impossible, so you turned your roar inward and kept it all inside.

Maybe you've even come to believe you don't have a voice.

Maybe you struggle with feeling irrelevant. Like what you do doesn't matter. That you aren't seen or valued.

Rest assured, God does see you and you do matter!

> The LORD keeps watch over you as you come and go, both now and forever. (Psalm 121:8 NLT)

He knows you, and he has plans for you!

> For we are his workmanship, created in Christ Jesus for good works, which God prepared beforehand, that we should walk in them. (Ephesians 2:10 ESV)

Sister, you have a voice. And it's one we need to hear. It's a voice given to you to share. In fact, there's never been such a need for your voice as at this moment. That's why we put this book together.

Miss Kay and I get to meet a lot of women. We see a lot of loneliness answered by the false promises of the world. To fill the holes in their hearts, they often seek fulfillment in the angry "empowerment" of feminism, expensive self-help "guru" training, or untold dollars spent on beauty and fashion.

Books like Sheryl Sandberg's *Lean In* challenge women to take on more initiative in business. Yes, we want women to win in their careers. But work is only one aspect of life. What we want for you, sister, is *abundant* life.

The world just keeps telling you to work harder, do more, be better. In fact, there are too many voices telling you what to do, right? And they're all talking at once, each one louder than the next. They're on social media, on TV, in online videos, on sold-out stages, and in the pages of books. Ironically, with so many ways to "connect," loneliness is a huge problem. So much so that the surgeon general of the United States declared loneliness an "epidemic."[2]

Kay and I travel a lot, and we've witnessed this epidemic firsthand. As we speak with audiences across the country, we meet incredible women. Once they hear our stories, they're emboldened to tell us their own—sometimes sharing things they've never, ever shared before.

We've heard some heartbreaking stories. Stories of girls growing up in broken homes; of physical, emotional, and sexual abuse; of addiction to sex and drugs; of the heartbreak of abortion; of marriage vows broken; of girls caught up in prostitution and sex trafficking. The list goes on and on.

It's worth saying here that sin doesn't happen in a vacuum. We know this from experience and from God's Word. At first it often seems like sin—going outside God's will—only hurts one person: the sinner. But sin's toxic splatter cannot be contained. The collateral damage of sin is unending. Unchecked and unconfessed, sin just keeps contaminating, sometimes for generations.

As we've talked with women, we've heard how the mistakes they've made and those made long before them pile up. Shame and guilt hem them in. It's like being in a house fire with flames licking at you from all sides. Cornered and stuck, you may even wonder if it's worth living anymore. Some even attempt suicide. Our hearts bleed for these women. Again, their stories hit too close to home.

We have heard some wild stories, but none wilder than the ones we've lived. As we'll share further along in this book, we get it. We have been there in more ways than one. A huge portion of our healing has come from making some of the same mistakes, suffering the same hurts, walking the same difficult road to recovery. And thereby we are able to encourage others.

We want to bring sisters who struggle home with us. To pray with them and for them. To feed them and teach them what the Word has to say about them. And often we do just that. Kay and I share our stories, we counsel, we pray with and for them, and we love on as many women as possible. We want our sisters to know they aren't alone. We want to show them a better way. More than anything, we want them to know the great mercy and love of the One who poured out mercy and love so unselfishly on the cross.

We've seen miracles. Sins confessed. Lives transformed. Marriages redeemed. We watch in awe when lonesomeness is defeated, replaced with holy sisterhood, and a mighty roar emerges. When thirsty souls receive living water, it's a beautiful thing. That's not to say the devil is never heard from again, but knowing that Jesus always wins gives us confidence. He defeated sin and death. The battle has already been won. Praise God!

We find it interesting that after lots of years of ministering to women, we have seen many similar themes emerge in the heartbreaks. We've also seen themes develop in the ways God speaks to these heartbreaks and redeems them. Since we can't always meet one-on-one, we decided to pick up our pens and write, in effect, this love letter to you, our sisters.

Maybe you read that last bit and said, "Okay, sure, but my life's not as bad as all that." And well, maybe not. But there's a reason you reached for this book. We don't believe in coincidences. Do you?

In our lives, Kay and I have learned that the only way to fix what's broken is Jesus.

We watch in awe when lonesomeness is defeated, replaced with holy sisterhood, and a mighty roar emerges.

> The Spirit of the Lord is upon Me,
> Because He has anointed Me
> To preach the gospel to the poor;
> He has sent Me to heal the brokenhearted,
> To proclaim liberty to the captives
> And recovery of sight to the blind,
> To set at liberty those who are oppressed;
> To proclaim the acceptable year of the Lord.
> (Luke 4:18–19 NKJV)

I tried to dress up my lack of relationship with Jesus for years, and it simply does not work. You have to bring it all to him. Be ready to own the story and bring it to him to redeem. That's when your roar begins to emerge.

We want women to find their voices and use them for the glory of God. We want them to tap into the blessing of community and enlarge their circles of influence with hospitality as never before. We aren't interested in self-help (helping one's self). Instead, we're hoping to usher in a revival of God's people. We imagine a day when women of faith cheer each other on and support each other in the everyday. With each of our individual roars going up, we'll create a collective roar that will shake the nations!

You have a story, and the world needs to hear it. The circumstances of your life have made and will continue to make your roar deeper, more authentic. None of us has had an easy life, and when you get down to it, no such thing exists! As Jesus himself said, "In the world you will have tribulation; but be of good cheer, I have overcome the world" (John 16:33 NKJV).

Real life includes the joys you've celebrated as well as the sadness you've endured. So go ahead and know that your roar will be made up of your best moments and your worst ones. The questions you've asked and the answers you've found. The battles you've fought and the ones you're still fighting—as well as the defeats you've had to accept.

Maybe your roar will be loud and confident, or it may be soft and sweet, depending on your personality. It might have the sound of spoken words, or maybe it will be expressed in some other way—through what you paint; how you love your family; the way you sing, dance, do people's taxes, or host a terrific party. Your roar will laugh sometimes and cry like a baby other times. It can comfort, it can correct, and it can communicate healthy choices and boundaries as needed. It will cheer from the stands or speak boldly when you're standing up for yourself or someone else. Sometimes it will cry out to God in desperation and other times in ecstatic praise.

With the passing of years, with God's grace, your roar will become a trusted source of wisdom, experience, and love for other sisters.

We've seen firsthand how a roar will change over time. Time and experience bring about growth. In the pages that follow, we will share how we once had a particular sound that now sounds very different. In my case, my voice was once harsh and even nasty. Since then God has given me a compassionate, tender sound that comes across as more of a meow than a roar.

There were years when Miss Kay hardly made a sound at all except to agree with what people told her. No more! She's since learned to use her voice quite well! We'll have much more to say about this later, but as you read the book, you'll see that our voices have changed—thanks be to God.

We believe yours will too.

One of our favorite things about a roar is how it can serve as an invitation, a chance to let yourself be known. Great relationships start with making yourself available. Your roar is something you'll discover deep within and express in your own special way. Others may hear it or see it in tangible ways, but most of the time they'll perceive it with their own hearts.

Healthy community will be born when you express your roar and hear the roars of others. You'll discover a place of sisterhood where you can be yourself and be loved for who you are. In turn, you'll offer your sisters a chance to be loved for who they are too.

Much like lions in a pride, you can create a safe place for growth and encouragement, where sisters can ask each other important questions and can offer honest, loving feedback. Where when one sister's energy is low, others can lend theirs. Where sisters can support and applaud one another. That's the blessing of sisterhood.

All right, Lisa, with all this talk about sisters, I (Kay) have to jump in and let people know we're not anti men. Sisters, I

Healthy community will be born when you express your roar and hear the roars of others.

love men! I've been married to the same man for more than fifty years. Together we have four grown sons. And Si, Phil's brother, is really like my own brother. So it's safe to say I'm very comfortable with men. Don't get the idea that we're only interested in women.

As sisters who share so much in common, we've seen what sisterhood in Christ can look like. It's something too good to keep to ourselves! But that doesn't mean we don't value men. We're forever grateful to God for our husbands, sons-in-law, and the other wonderful men in our family and in our larger family, the church. Our culture right now is so pro-women that there is almost an overcorrection. It can even be anti-male. That makes no sense. Besides, we're positive it's not biblical. God made men. He made us distinctly different from them. That was no mistake on God's part. So, while we honor and appreciate men, this book isn't about them. It's about the special blessing that comes—for us and for you—from great relationships with our sisters.

That's right, Miss Kay. There's something extra special about female friendships. Like us—we're connected as mother-in-law and daughter-in-law, and we share a deep and true friendship that has been severely tested. (Y'all are getting ready to read about that in the pages of this book.) We've both experienced heartbreak, abuse, shame, loneliness, and desperation. We've had to make difficult choices. And, by God's grace, we've experienced healing, restoration, joy, and a sense of purpose that makes each day a great adventure.

As you'll discover later in our story, we've been pleasantly surprised by some of the sisters we've met along the way. Some more surprising than others.

Anyway, chances are, something in Kay's and my stories will probably connect with you. We often hear, "That's like what happened with me!" We have found that to be true for many, many women as we befriend, encourage, and help them find their roar. Every sister matters. Whether we're supporting her through a difficult season privately over a slice of Miss Kay's pie, teaching her in a class, or leading her in a small group at church; whether we're sharing our stories with large audiences or passing along an important life lesson or a good influence through reruns of our family's *Duck Dynasty* television show, the desire of our hearts is to see each woman live an abundant life in Jesus. We love to hear women roar!

We want to hear you roar. So, are you ready to live your best, most fulfilled life?

Are you ready to discover your voice and express your uniqueness so the real you can shine forth?

Are you ready for deep, healthy relationships with other women?

Okay, then, sister, you're ready to roar.

1

Made to Roar

God's Heart for Your Unique Story

Tell every nation on earth,
"The LORD is wonderful
and does marvelous things!"

1 CHRONICLES 16:24 CEV

Where we live by the Ouachita River, a sound lifts up to the sky around sunset. It's not the sound from a big cat, but it's a roar all right. After you've gotten used to the volume, you'll start to pick out different individual sounds. A low-throated bullfrog. The whir of cicadas. High-pitched tree crickets. It's a kind of symphony of bullfrogs, crickets, cicadas, and katydids in the cypress trees. You might hear an armadillo rustling through the leaves on the ground, a wolf howling, or squirrels running in the trees overhead. Sometimes you'll hear snakes slithering along or rattling their tails.

It's noisy, and it's a lot to take in at first. But we like it.

Maybe that riverside roar is like what God hears when he's listening to his children from heaven. What might otherwise sound like random noise is music to the Father. After all, he made this whole wide world—the rivers, the lakes, the oceans, and everything on land and sea and in the air. He made us—you and Miss Kay and me. "[God] knit me together in my mother's womb" (Psalm 139:13). And he calls each of us his own.

Like all those riverside creatures, we've each been given a voice. God didn't give us voices by accident—not at all! God doesn't do anything by accident. As the apostle Paul put it in Ephesians 2:10, "We are God's masterpiece. He has created us anew in Christ Jesus, so we can do the good things he planned for us long ago" (NLT).

Whoa! Not only are we God's masterpiece, but we have a voice on purpose and for a purpose. That purpose was planned by God eons ago. That's pretty special—and maybe even a bit intimidating.

Think of it: you're unique, created by God to be your original self, and created by him on purpose to make a difference.

What's Your Story?

Every sister has a story to tell. I do, Kay does, and you do. It's the narrative of how you got to this moment in time, how you became the woman you are right this moment. Your story is a rich, complicated fabric woven from delights and heartbreaks, successes and failures, good decisions and poor choices. It includes the moments when everything worked out exactly as planned and the times when everything fell apart.

And let's not forget suffering. I know you've suffered, or you wouldn't be reading this book. If we didn't suffer, we wouldn't be human—and we sure wouldn't have character. Romans 5:3–5 says that "suffering produces perseverance; perseverance, character; and character, hope. And hope does not put us to shame, because God's love has been poured out into our hearts through the Holy Spirit, who has been given to us."

Let's be clear: we're not fans of suffering. It is not fun to go through painful periods. But the struggles and the dark times are what refine us.

Before we go farther in this book, know this: whatever your story is, you're welcome here. I can assure you that your

Your past does not determine your future.

story wouldn't shock us. We've seen a lot, we've heard a lot, and we've personally *lived* a lot. With Kay and me, you're in a safe place—a place that's safe to explore your heart, safe to be honest about yourself, safe to ask for God's forgiveness and help, and safe to dream of a better life. After all, our Savior, Jesus, came so that you could have life and have it "more abundantly" (John 10:10 NKJV).

In fact, our hope is that this book will help you enter into that abundance. We understand how it feels to look toward the future and see question marks. To feel like you've made too many mistakes. To feel like there's a black hole threatening to pull you back in. Take courage. Simply picking up this book and reading it is a step in the right direction, a step toward hope, healing, strength, and a better future than you ever thought possible. Each step makes the next one easier, helping you feel a bit braver and more confident.

It's time to be the strong, unique woman God created you to be—the peace-filled, loving, happy, loved, full-of-potential woman he sees when he looks at you. As you keep moving forward, by God's grace, you will step right into your roar. Know this: your past does not determine your future. In fact, it set the stage for a greater life than you could ever imagine.

We want to help women like you find their voices and use them for God's glory. We want to help them tap into the blessing of community. And we want to empower them to enlarge their circle of influence with hospitality as never before.

Again, we aren't interested in self-help methods. Instead, we want to point women to the ultimate help: Jesus. We want our lives to point women to him! The best thing we can hope for is a revival of God's people. We imagine a day when sisters in the faith cheer each other on and support each other day in and day out. With each of our individual roars that go up, our collective roar will shake the nations! With God's help, we will roar our way right into heaven—together.

God is ready to turn the painful parts of your past into a roar.

Most of us have something in our past we deeply regret. Something we did or something that was done to us. A wound or scar, a pain, a problem. Many of us have scars or fresh wounds from something that happened years or hours ago. We live with a pain that sometimes subsides but never goes away. With a shame that won't wash off, no matter how hot the water. If that's you, welcome to the Sister Roar sisterhood.

Consider what Scripture says:

> We know that in all things God works for the good of those who love him, who have been called according to his purpose. (Romans 8:28)

If your past is a series of disappointments, pains, and heartbreaks, God can turn it into a source of joy. Your story can help others find clarity, and your bad choices may help someone else make the right ones. Though your past may be a source of shame, in Christ you can find total forgiveness and peace—and you can help someone else unload her burden of condemnation.

You don't need to hide from your past or try to forget it. And you can't ignore it or pretend it never existed. Instead, it's time to own it. Embrace it. Forgive yourself or others for

If your past is a series of disappointments, pains, and heartbreaks, God can turn it into a source of joy.

anything that needs to be forgiven. Position yourself to have your hurts healed, and let God use your story in a positive way.

If you'll let us, we'd like to share part of our stories to show you what we're talking about. Kay and I have the common denominator of becoming pregnant as teenagers. But Kay and I made totally different choices. I had an abortion, which I'll talk about later in the book. Kay chose to carry her child to term, give birth, and raise him.

Because of our shared history, Kay and I each have a tender spot in our hearts for women experiencing unplanned pregnancies. We both publicly advocate for pro-life causes, and privately we gravitate toward women in desperate situations—those wondering what to do and where to turn. We counsel young mothers, pray with them, and help them find the practical resources and support they need while working closely with our local crisis pregnancy center.

We have been there. We know the fear and feelings of anxiety that an unexpected pregnancy can bring about. We also know what a great blessing an unplanned baby can be. After all, Kay's son Al became my husband!

Some women choose to have an abortion. I know all too well the thoughts and emotions that lead to this choice. I can close my eyes and instantly remember the sights and smells and sounds I experienced that day. And I know the emotions that follow. When I speak with a woman contemplating abortion, I'm mindful of all these realities. It's not just an intellectual connection. I have deep compassion as I speak the truth to her. Because of the way God touched my life years after I chose to terminate my pregnancy, and because of the beliefs I now hold,

I am a champion for life. My strong desire is to spare women the ugly, long-lasting consequences of abortion. That's part of my roar.

This is just one example of how God redeems our pasts and makes them part of our roars. We'll share more—wait till you hear how much more—but this unflattering story illustrates in a practical way how God is ready to use *every* story for good.

When You've Hurt Someone You Love

As a young wife and mother, in 1989, life was good for me—not perfect, but good. I had my share of stresses along with many blessings. I was married to Al, whom I'd fallen in love with at first sight in the sixth grade. We had two beautiful daughters and a large, happy extended Robertson family we lived close to and saw often. Al worked for Duck Commander, and I had a good job at a local loan company.

When I became romantically attracted to a man who had been nothing more than an acquaintance for several years, I was surprised. At the time, my marriage was strained for various reasons, so I was frustrated and discontent, but an extramarital relationship was not my intention. Unexpected job circumstances brought this man into my life on a regular basis, and soon we were involved in an emotional affair that never became sexual but definitely fell into the category of "unfaithfulness."

After Al found out about it, he forgave me. I was extremely relieved. I was so thankful I did not lose my marriage or my family over that situation. The instruction I remember giving myself every time I thought about it was, "You'd better not *ever* do this again." In addition, I could not shake what Al had said to me when he discovered this relationship: "If you ever do anything like this again, I *will* divorce you!" And I believed him.

I knew how deeply I had hurt Al and others, and I was determined not to let that happen again. What I did not know was that God could help me change my life. I thought it was all up to me and my will, which was admittedly weak. Al expected me to stay faithful, and I expected fidelity from myself. But I did not have the resources—the experience, the teaching, the personal relationship with God, the wisdom of a skilled counselor, or other means of support—that would help me become the kind of wife we hear about in marriage vows, who, "forsaking all others," clings only to her husband.

Nine years later, in 1998, I fell into the same trap of the Enemy, Satan. By that time, Duck Commander's business had grown, and I worked there for Phil and Kay. When I answered the phone one day, I was shocked to hear the voice of one of my high school boyfriends, a man I had not seen in years. I had no idea that I could fall for him again. The Enemy, on the other hand, was well aware of the possibility and skillfully laid his trap.

When I recognized those old feelings of attraction to a man who was not my husband, I thought I could resist them. I could not. I let him win me over. That relationship was a full-blown affair, and over time it did become sexual.

In addition to everything else I did wrong, I lied about this relationship. I lied to Al, to my family and friends, and even to myself. So, if you have ever found yourself caught in such a web of trouble or sin and then lied about it, I get it. I know the fear and the feeling of desperation of not being able to tell the truth. It's a nightmare, and it feels hopeless. I'm here to give you hope and to offer a helping hand.

Later I'll share more about my past and explain many of the reasons I was vulnerable to the relationship that had happened nine years earlier and to this extramarital affair. But for now, let me stay focused on one important point: I know what it's like to give in to temptation, make mistakes, make foolish and sinful choices. I understand what it's like to think you will lose your friends and perhaps your family. To think that you will be branded for life with the mark of your mistake. My heart goes out to my sister who wonders if she can ever overcome and move beyond "what happened" or "that situation."

I have good news: she can. *You* can.

My sin deeply wounded the people I love most. Maybe you can relate. Maybe you've also hurt the ones you love. It's a hard pain to get past, but it is possible, and I know that with God's help you can do it. I can assure you of this because *every single one of the relationships I damaged has been restored* and is now better than ever.

Specifically, Kay was furious with me for cheating on her son. She had every right to be. But the pain of her past compelled her to have compassion on me. The full force of her love and protective heart toward Alan could have raged against me, and had she chosen to respond that way, I would have understood. But she didn't. She was hurt and she was upset, but she continued to treat me better than I could have imagined possible. For this and for countless other reasons, I owe her a debt of gratitude I will never be able to repay. She is a big part of the reason I was able to recover. God used Miss Kay and her unconditional love in powerful ways to help me out of the muck and mire of sin and into a wonderful present and a hope-filled future.

We share this story and others to bring home the point that you don't have to stay stuck in the past. We've just shared the tip of the iceberg of our own pasts, so that you can know they're not all pretty. But by God's grace, the past is behind us. God has used our experiences to shape us into stronger women. He has given us hearts for the struggling and the hopeless. Our voices vibrate with hope because at times all we had was hope. Nothing seemed sure. Good things were not guaranteed. But God can take even the tiniest spark of hope in the midst of dark circumstances and turn a life completely around. We want to help you find that spark.

To move from the past in a healthy way, we can't pretend the past never happened. We can't stuff it deep in our hearts and forget about it. We'll go into this later, but for now, let's just say we must face the reality of the past, feel the emotion of it, and make the bold decision to hope and to believe God can make something good from it.

There is no brokenness God cannot mend, no ugly situation he cannot make beautiful, no sadness he cannot turn to joy. God will redeem what you hand over to him. Maybe you are skeptical. Maybe you've never seen God totally transform a life. That's okay.

We're not experts, we're just blessed to be in the right

There is no brokenness God cannot mend, no ugly situation he cannot make beautiful, no sadness he cannot turn to joy.

family—the royal family of God. What we aim to share with you is based on our life experiences and the treasures we've discovered in the Word of God.

> Everything in the Scriptures is God's Word. All of it is useful for teaching and helping people and for correcting them and showing them how to live. (2 Timothy 3:16 CEV)

There's nothing in life that the Word doesn't address. So we're going to draw on God's Word to help you find your voice and use it for God's glory, to tap into the blessings of community, and to enlarge your circle of sisterhood.

The Power of Hope

There is not a woman on the planet who has not at some time found herself stuck in a bad situation. People might judge her and say, "Why doesn't she do something to change her life if it's so bad?" I learned a long time ago not to judge. What any of us needs in times like that isn't judgment; it's hope.

In Louisiana we eat a lot of crawfish. In spring and summer especially, Phil and the boys will catch a bunch and bring them home for a good old-fashioned crawfish broil. The first thing you do is put them into an ice bath. The cold keeps them alive so we can wash them. They don't seem to mind the cold—it's not uncomfortable. It's the pot of boiling water they hate. You have to put a lid on quick or they'll jump right out! Now, I don't know this from experience, but I hear that if you put crawfish in a pot of cool water and turn up the heat slowly, you don't even need to keep a lid on. With a more gradual change in temperature, the danger isn't apparent until it's too late.

Like I said, I never tried that personally. I do know, however, what it feels like to gradually lose hope. And I've seen it happen too often. I've seen women put up with something that gets worse over time. They might think at first, *He's jealous. He yells some, but his bark is worse than his bite.* Next thing you know it's, *If I can just figure out a way to make him happy, things will get better.* Then the troubles pile up, until a woman gets tired in her bones and change feels out of reach.

I wonder if that's how it was for the woman we read about in Luke 8.

Scripture doesn't give us her name, but it does give us some pretty specific details. We learn she'd been suffering for a long time—twelve years. That's how long she'd been hemorrhaging blood. Losing blood makes you feel weak, like you don't have any energy. Just imagine how exhausted this poor woman must have been after twelve years.

I say poor, but she must have had resources, because she was able to pay for the help of doctors. Those doctors took her money, Scripture says, but they didn't help one little bit. In fact, after they did their thing, she was worse than ever. Think about that. She was already feeling rotten, and then these charlatans promised to help but only made things worse. She "suffered" in their care (Mark 5:26). When you give all you can and you're worse off than before, it's downright discouraging. Sick, taken advantage of, tired, and hopeless—that's the state this woman was in when she heard something hopeful. She heard about

Jesus, who had cast out demons, healed a paralyzed man, and done many other miracles. When she heard this, she knew right away he had the power to heal her.

Now, keep in mind that Jesus was a rabbi—a teacher of Jewish law. And Jewish law said that women who were bleeding were ceremonially unclean. So any woman who was bleeding should have been steering clear of crowds. At minimum, anyone who knew she was bleeding would avoid her, which would be pretty humiliating. But they might do even worse; they might punish her.

What could she do? She wasn't supposed to be out and about. She didn't want to be a bother or a distraction. In humility—maybe even trying to avoid detection—she decided to try to sneak up and touch Jesus. In faith, she thought if she could at least do that, she'd be healed.

So she did. She snuck up, reached out, and touched his robe—and *bam*, she felt herself heal!

Scripture says she was healed immediately.

> Now a woman, having a flow of blood for twelve years, who had spent all her livelihood on physicians and could not be healed by any, came from behind and touched the border of His garment. And immediately her flow of blood stopped.
>
> And Jesus said, "Who touched Me?"
>
> When all denied it, Peter and those with him said, "Master, the multitudes throng and press You, and You say, 'Who touched Me?'"
>
> But Jesus said, "Somebody touched Me, for I perceived power going out from Me."

> Now when the woman saw that she was not hidden, she came trembling; and falling down before Him, she declared to Him in the presence of all the people the reason she had touched Him and how she was healed immediately.
>
> And He said to her, "Daughter, be of good cheer; your faith has made you well. Go in peace." (Luke 8:43–48 NKJV)

Can you imagine this woman's joy? Her relief? Her hope? After being disappointed time and again by those who promised one thing and delivered another, she was whole!

But wait. Jesus stopped in his tracks. He asked, "Who touched me?" She'd succeeded in part—she was healed—but she was not so successful in keeping a low profile.

What came next shows the woman's courage. Though she'd felt desperate, drained, and depressed just moments before, now she felt whole and hopeful. Even though she was afraid of what might happen, she faced her fear. She stepped out of the crowd and told Jesus "the whole truth" (Mark 5:33). Then Jesus looked directly at her and said, "Daughter . . . your faith has made you well. Go in peace " (Luke 8:48 NKJV).

Living in fear of the law, the woman probably expected punishment. What she got was mercy and grace. Also, notice how Jesus called her "daughter." This was especially kind of Jesus. She had to have felt like an old woman after all her suffering, and here Jesus spoke to her gently, paternally, even though he was likely just thirty-two.

Then he went on his way, off to (literally) raise the dead.

Seems to me that Jesus called this woman out on purpose for two reasons. He wanted to personally interact with her. He's so relational! I also think he wanted her to witness in front of all those people. He not only healed her but invited her to use her voice—her testimony—when she had been denied a voice for too long. She'd been taken advantage of and marginalized. Jesus' power redeemed her and gave her freedom, wholeness, and life!

I believe he's inviting you and me to do the same today.

Your Turn

- Is your story something you are open about, or do you keep it inside?
- Have you offered it to God yet? Has he redeemed it?
- Who do you envision sharing your story with? What outcome do you hope for?
- What has kept you from telling your story?
- If you have shared your story, who did you share it with? What was the outcome?

2

Hungry, Hungry, Hungry

Satisfy the Cravings of Your Heart

The righteous eats to the satisfying of his soul,
But the stomach of the wicked shall be in want.

PROVERBS 13:25 NKJV

The Robertson house is a good place to be if you're hungry. Our family has a reputation for good food. And with good reason: Kay has made an art out of feeding people.

That's right, Lisa. Not a day goes by that somebody doesn't ask for one of my signature dishes: chicken and dumplings, fried corn bread, pork roast with dumplings, spaghetti with meat sauce, fried apple pies, homemade crawfish pie, or homemade shrimp pie. I make the best homemade piecrust and biscuits too. We'll have film crews out to the house, and sometimes I'll feed the whole bunch of them—breakfast, lunch, and dinner. There's always plenty to share. I cook like I'm feeding an army. Over the years, Phil and the boys would bring home friends. I'd feed them, and Phil would share the gospel with them. Nobody ever left our house with an empty belly or not hearing the gospel.

Some folks live with what's called "food insecurity." They're not sure where they'll get their next meal. When I sense somebody feels that way, I keep the food on the table and in plain sight. That keeps them from feeling anxious. It's better for their digestion—and their spirit—if they know they can eat all they want.

Personally I've never worried about going hungry. I have gone without money, for sure, but my parents owned the only grocery store in Ida, Louisiana, our little town. It was called Carroway's General Store. I never had to worry about not having enough to eat. Plus my father's mother, Nanny, had an incredible garden, and we could always get fresh food from right out there in the yard. Then I married the best hunter and fisherman in Louisiana. So, even when times were lean, there was always something for me to cook. Phil would see to it.

I have, however, felt hungry for something I couldn't name. For the first ten years of our marriage, Phil was running with the devil. That made me feel desperate and anxious in a different way. I kept thinking that if he'd just quit drinking and stay home, I'd be happy. But he just kept getting further and further into his lifestyle—drinking and running around, going off for days at a time and leaving me and the boys alone.

One night he came home drunk, mean, and ready for a fight. He even accused me of running around on him, which was ridiculous. When would I have had the time? With a full-time job and three little kids and a house to take care of I barely had time to sleep! But since he was being unfaithful to me, his wild idea was that I was too. I couldn't believe it. We argued and argued, fought and fought. Finally, I went into the bathroom and locked the door. I was bone-tired. I thought, *I just wish I could take something and go to sleep for a long, long time.*

That's when I heard the footsteps of our three little boys. I'll never forget that sound of their little feet on the floor, coming up to that door. Alan had been going to church and loved the Lord. He said, "Don't worry, Momma. God will help us." Something in me knew he was right. I'd been looking for help in the wrong place. I decided to take the boys to church by myself. I started following the Lord as best I could. I realized the truth in Proverbs 13:12: "Hope deferred makes the heart sick, but when the desire comes, it is a tree of life" (NKJV).

It got to where the kids and I talked about Jesus so much that Phil kicked us out. He said I was "ruining his life" with all my talking about God and my newfound faith. That was a turning point. My perspective shifted. I stopped trying to get Phil to change. I wanted God to change *me*. I became hungry for his Word.

The Bible talks about hunger a lot.

The hunger of the Israelites in the wilderness.

The hunger of the five thousand who sat down to listen to Jesus and then got fed.

The disciples who figured out where the best fish were, thanks to Jesus' instruction.

The disciples eating with Jesus by a beachside campfire after his resurrection.

And God regularly reminds us to feed the hungry (Isaiah 58:10). I've witnessed Kay doing this more times than I can count. It's a talent and a calling and part of her unique roar.

Meeting someone's need for food is a good thing. But the Bible also talks about a hunger that goes way down deep in the soul, like Kay was talking about.

The psalmist David wrote, "My soul thirsts for God, for the living God. When shall I come and appear before God?"

Through his life, death, and resurrection, Jesus imparted to us the Holy Spirit—so that we will never be without God, not even for a second!

(Psalm 42:2 NKJV). And "He satisfies the longing soul, and the *hungry soul* he fills with good things" (Psalm 107:9 ESV, emphasis added).

Jesus fulfills the soul's longings for God. He promises that only he himself will satisfy. "I am the bread of life; whoever comes to me shall not hunger, and whoever believes in me shall never thirst" (John 6:35 ESV). Through his life, death, and resurrection, Jesus imparted to us the Holy Spirit—so that we will never be without God, not even for a second!

That kind of hunger haunted the woman Jesus encountered in John 4.

High Noon at the Well

> Now Jesus learned that the Pharisees had heard that he was gaining and baptizing more disciples than John—although in fact it was not Jesus who baptized, but his disciples. So he left Judea and went back once more to Galilee.
>
> Now he had to go through Samaria. So he came to a town in Samaria called Sychar, near the plot of ground Jacob had given to his son Joseph. Jacob's well was there, and Jesus, tired as he was from the journey, sat down by the well. It was about noon. (John 4:1–6)

I've never been to the Middle East, but the noonday sun can be uncomfortably hot in Louisiana, so I imagine that when Jesus was at the well that day, it was pretty hot. Why would a woman come to draw water then of all times? Maybe she was trying to avoid crowds that gathered there in the cool of the morning. Maybe she was hiding, hoping to avoid the whispers. Or it could be that she'd slept in. She might have had a late night. Scripture doesn't tell us.

Jesus saw her there alone and asked her for a drink of water. She was surprised for a couple of reasons. She was an unmarried woman, and it was inappropriate for them to converse. Also, she was a Samaritan and he was a Jew. Samaritans and Jews didn't get along. What's more, Jesus was a teacher of the law—a rabbi—and a respected member of Jewish society. Any drink she might have given him would have been seen by his peers as "ceremonially unclean."

She called him out on this.

> "You are a Jew and I am a Samaritan woman. How can you ask me for a drink?" (For Jews do not associate with Samaritans.)
>
> Jesus answered her, "If you knew the gift of God and who it is that asks you for a drink, you would have asked him and he would have given you living water." (vv. 9–10)

Can you imagine her confusion? They shouldn't have been talking, and yet what he said intrigued her. And honestly, she got a little sassy about it.

> "You have nothing to draw with and the well is deep. Where can you get this living water? Are you greater than our father Jacob, who gave us the well and drank from it himself, as did also his sons and his livestock?" (vv. 11–12)

Is it me or does it seem like she had her back up here? It's as if she was asking, "Who do you think you are, mister?"

> Jesus answered, "Everyone who drinks this water will be thirsty again, but whoever drinks the water I give them will never thirst. Indeed, the water I give them will become in them a spring of water welling up to eternal life."
>
> The woman said to him, "Sir, give me this water so that I won't get thirsty and have to keep coming here to draw water."
>
> He told her, "Go, call your husband and come back."
>
> "I have no husband," she replied. (vv. 13–17)

I can relate to this. It hurts to have to say something like this out loud. To confess something painful, hurtful, and yet a reality. But Jesus was not surprised. *He already knew this and more*. Look at what he said next:

> "You are right when you say you have no husband. The fact is, you have had five husbands, and the man you now have is not your husband." (v. 18)

Whoa. That must have been disconcerting. Yet Jesus had the facts straight. She'd been living in sin and getting in deeper and deeper, with no prospects, no future. That kind of clarity must have taken her breath away. Jesus had her attention. I love this part.

> "A time is coming and has now come when the true worshipers will worship the Father in the Spirit and in truth, for

> they are the kind of worshipers the Father seeks. God is spirit, and his worshipers must worship in the Spirit and *in truth*."
>
> The woman said, "I know that Messiah" (called Christ) "is coming. When he comes, he will explain everything to us."
>
> Then Jesus declared, "I, the one speaking to you—I am he." (vv. 23–26, emphasis added)

Can you imagine? "I, the one speaking . . . am he." This is the biggest news ever, and she's the first to know! The woman with the past, the woman with no prospects, the woman avoiding company.

She got so excited she stopped what she was doing and went back to town *to tell everyone*. She even forgot her jar. Back in town she told folks about Jesus. The very people she'd been avoiding, she was seeking. "Come and see!" she said. She was the spokesperson to the whole town based on one conversation with Jesus.

Jesus knew this woman was hiding and yet that her heart desperately longed to be seen. Their brief conversation must have fed her. Can you imagine how *seen* she felt? To be spoken to with respect and hope and love? The result was nothing less than complete transformation.

Their meeting was not accidental. It was arranged by divine design. Jesus, on his way to deliver the gospel to the Jews, stopped and loved one woman, and a whole bunch of other people were saved as a result. Isn't that beautiful?

At her lowest point, she met Jesus and stepped into her purpose: to deliver the gospel. Jesus knew this woman better than she knew herself. That's always true, isn't it? He knows what

[Jesus] knows what we need before we know it. He has plans that would blow our minds if we knew them ahead of time!

we need before we know it. He has plans that would blow our minds if we knew them ahead of time!

Because of her eyewitness testimony, many were saved.

> Many of the Samaritans from that town believed in him because of the woman's testimony, "He told me everything I ever did." So when the Samaritans came to him, they urged him to stay with them, and he stayed two days. And because of his words many more became believers. They said to the woman, "We no longer believe just because of what you said; now we have heard for ourselves, and we know that this man really is the Savior of the world." (vv. 39–42)

When they met Jesus, they, too, believed. This woman's enthusiasm, candor, and conviction led many to salvation. She'd multiplied her own salvation by being willing to share her story.

What an amazing roar!

Jesus extends the offer of his living water to us as he did to that woman at the well. Check out this verse in Revelation, meant for you and me.

> The Spirit and the bride say, "Come!"
> Everyone who hears this should say, "Come!"
> If you are thirsty, come! If you want life-giving water,
> come and take it! It's free! (Revelation 22:17 CEV)

Having tasted living water, trying to quench a thirst any other way is like drinking from the Ouachita River. It's wet, all right, but it's not good for drinking!

Kay's gut-level hunger motivated her to make a life change. She wanted more for her family, more for herself—that's why she turned her life over to God. And it made all the difference. It wasn't a quick fix. In the short term, it was painful when Phil kicked her and the kids out of the house. But ultimately Phil decided to follow Jesus too. The rest, as they say, is history.

Change requires a lot of energy, doesn't it? I know this from experience, and I know you do too, sister! It can wear a girl out. Caffeine can only get us so far. God has wired a divine motivator into us that kicks in when we hunger for something beyond our current experience. It gives us energy to pursue him. That motivator is *desire*. God created desire. It's not a bad thing. But we get messed up when we believe something other than God can satisfy our desire for him! We say, "I'll be satisfied when . . ."

We think that if we can gather enough money, then we'll be satisfied. This can be an unspoken desire, a subtle discontent, or an overt goal. *When I get* x *amount of money, I'll be happy.* Or maybe that if we have the money to buy certain things—like a new house or a better car or a better education—those things will bring us the happiness we so crave.

Some of us are hungry for fame. The thought is, *I'd be happy if more people liked me*. Social media is especially addictive this way. We all know how it feels when we post something and get that one like—we want more. Where's the next one? When will I get another friend request? And another? It's a new twist on the idea we had once that becoming popular will make us happy. It's our longing to connect.

I saw a billboard for a wireless internet provider that said they promise to make customers feel "connected." What a great example of a distortion of truth. Yes, God wired us for communion with him and others, but social media and the internet is not real connection. Not on a heart and soul level. The truth is, you can have thousands of followers and still be lonely. You can fill stadiums as a performer and still be lonely.

Speaking of connection, some women might be hungry for sex. We think sex will satisfy us. Maybe more or better sex, that will do it for us. That will make us happy, right?

These things—money, fame, and sex—are blessings from God.

> Every good and perfect gift is from above, coming down from the Father of the heavenly lights, who does not change like shifting shadows. (James 1:17)

Sometimes, however, we seek the gift instead of the Giver. When that happens, we've made the gift an idol. That's when things go sideways. We worship the gift when the truth is that only God can satisfy.

"More, More, More!"

Some of us experience hunger as more of an itch than an idol. In other words, we're not so much *focused* on it as we are *distracted* by it. It's a sense of self-reliance that says, *If I can just do things a certain way, I'll be at peace.* Here are some of the ways the "itch" of hunger manifests.

- **Getting stuff done.** This is the mentality that says, *I am so busy!* Often what's going on is that we're trying to drown out our feelings with activity and productivity. This craving can be disguised as a desire to be productive, or even career or family-values focus.
- **Pushing to be healthy, healthy, healthy.** This mentality says, *If my body is healthy, I'll be happy.* Women and men can suffer from this, but it's more complicated for women because our culture supplies complex messages about body image. Though our bodies are temples of the Holy Spirit, they're mortal. And we can become preoccupied with trying to perfect them.
- **Striving for perfection.** Kay and I both often hear this refrain: "I'm a control freak." It's a fallacy to think that if we controlled every aspect of our day, we'd be better off. We're too limited in our understanding and wisdom for that to be true! It's a good thing God is in control.
- **Desiring "happily ever after."** The desire for connection is God-given. The desire to be connected to a soul mate is legit. I get it. I used to think that having the perfect man would complete me too. That did not happen. When my "perfect man" said he wanted to marry me, I thought he would be my ticket to happiness. And yet, without a true relationship with God, I continued to live lost, trying to fill my emptiness in other ways. When we put someone else on a pedestal and think they can complete us, we will be disappointed.

Power, money, sex—these things aren't bad. If God wills, I hope you are the beneficiary of them all. But will they satisfy the longing of your soul?

The world says, "Girl, you can be happy. You just need to self-actualize! Wash your face and do your daily affirmations. Then you can make more money, perfect your looks and body, attract the 'perfect' partner who will meet all your needs—and, ta-da, you'll be living your best life!"

If you think that sounds fishy or suspicious, you're right! It's a boatload of baloney!

God's Word says it way simpler: only God can satisfy.

Jesus, who is Truth, promises abundant life. He promises peace. He promises joy. What he doesn't promise is happiness. In fact, he said, "Here on earth you *will* have many trials and sorrows" (John 16:33 NLT, emphasis added).

Sister, be encouraged! You will flourish and be fruitful in following Jesus. We pray you'll be filled with a knowledge of God's love for you. That you will experience God's power. That you will find your voice and use that voice for kingdom purposes, for the glory of the Lord and the salvation of many.

Happiness is part of all that, just as sunny days are a part of the weather. It's not always sunny, but it is sometimes. The point, sisters, is *holiness*.

> As the One who called you is holy, you also are to be holy in all your conduct; for it is written, Be holy, because I am holy. (1 Peter 1:15–16 HCSB)

Holy simply means set apart for God. It's a mindset of belonging to God, the Creator of the universe, who cares deeply about you, so much so that he knows how many hairs are on your head and asks you to surrender your dreams, desires, and thoughts to him. To be holy is to go about your life with the knowledge that Christ lives in you (Galatians 2:20). Joni Eareckson Tada says, "Holiness isn't in a style of dress. It's not a matter of rules and regulations. It's a way of life that emanates quietness and rest, joy in family, shared pleasures with friends, the help of a neighbor—and the hope of a Savior."[3]

That's why we "seek . . . his righteousness" (Matthew 6:33). It bothers me when people throw around the term *self-righteous* about Christians. It's not that I mind the insult. What's so wrong about it is that nobody is righteous through self-anything. There's nothing we can do to be righteous. Righteousness comes from God. Christ in you is the mystery of "godliness." I've tasted and seen that the Lord is good (Psalm 34:8). I know that only the Lord can satisfy.

God's Word regarding hunger: "God blesses those people who want to obey him more than to eat or drink. They will be given what they want!" (Matthew 5:6 CEV). So go on, be hungry and thirsty for righteousness. Scripture promises that those who hunger and thirst for righteousness will be satisfied!

It's beautiful how God takes all our mess and noise and weaves it into something special. God is the ultimate Creator. His ability to create something from my mess humbles me. His willingness to redeem never ceases to amaze me.

I'm redeemed—I'm not perfect. God is sanctifying me all

Every new relationship is a new opportunity for grace.

the time. Looking back, I can see how the refining he does in me almost always comes through my relationships. Those are the places my character is tested and tried most and where his grace seems to flow most.

It seems to me he made me part of this divine family so that I can participate in divine grace! I see it in my relationships with Al, my kids, my friends, and my family. Every new relationship is a new opportunity for grace.

One of the most unexpected and grace-filled relationships of my life came about in the most surprising way. Kay and I will share that with you in the next chapter.

Your Turn

- What's your experience with hunger?
- Have you experienced food insecurity or food disorders?
- Do you crave fame, fortune, and love?
- Have you ever placed inordinate pressure on yourself to achieve?
- Do you have any "idols" in your life?

3

Welcome to the Pride

Surrendered Hearts

The LORD directs the steps of the godly.
He delights in every detail of their lives.

PSALM 37:23 NLT

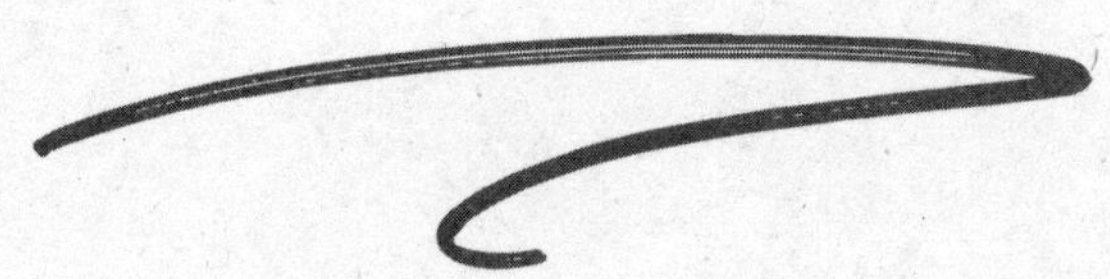

Kay and I watched as a bright pink sun sank into the ocean waves. The ocean's roar soothed my soul as we enjoyed the delicious crawfish casserole prepared by my sister-in-law. We were on our annual Robertson family vacation to the Gulf Coast. Gratitude bubbled up inside me. It was joy, pure and simple. I thanked God aloud with eyes wide open—not wanting to miss a moment of the glorious sunset. Seagulls squawked overhead. Children laughed and shouted to each other, splashing in the tide, racing to catch tiny minnows. I wondered, in the face of such majesty, how could anyone not believe in a Creator who masterfully weaves together such a world?

Scripture testifies that we are made on purpose, for a purpose (1 Peter 2:9). God the Father calls us his own and says he has plans to prosper and not harm us (Jeremiah 29:11). We proclaim this to be true by faith. We also see it play out over and over again in Scripture—in the accounts about the woman at the well, the woman desperate to touch Jesus' robe and be healed, Miriam, Elizabeth, Lydia, Esther, Ruth, Mary, and so many more. I see it in my own life and in the lives of those I love, don't you, Kay?

I do! When I see lives changed for the better, I know there's a God, because we simply cannot change ourselves. You and I both know that from personal experience.

The Enemy wants to mess with God's plans and our purpose. He's been at it since the beginning of time. Remember how he tried to tempt Jesus? Make no mistake, the devil hasn't given up. He is at it today, trying to get us to go against God's will. The good news is, victory has already been won through Jesus.

God generously invites us to participate in his redemption plan. We can participate even as it happens. It's as clear and beautiful as any sunset on the beach. Take, for example, the way God's plans and infinite creativity have unfolded in someone very dear to us. Her name is Phyllis, and I'm happy to introduce her. We don't want you to miss a word of her story, so we've invited Phyllis to tell it herself.

Phyllis's Story

I grew up going to church, loving the Lord. It's funny. Nobody else in my family went to church, but at age nine, somehow I'd get myself up on Sunday mornings and catch the church bus that came through our neighborhood. Being at church felt natural to me. I loved the songs we sang and the lessons we learned about Jesus and God's love. So at an early age, I asked Jesus to be my Lord and Savior. God's Word became very special to me. My family thought it was odd and didn't miss a chance to tell me so, but they never stood in my way.

Our home life was not what you'd call stable. At age thirteen, I moved in with my older sister and her boyfriend. That didn't last long. I soon moved in with a friend. I loved learning, so I graduated high school, went to college and then nursing school. I met my now-husband Tony while still in high school. Together we had two beautiful boys. We raised them to love the Lord, even serving as missionaries in Nicaragua for five years.

A few years ago, our oldest son took a DNA test to learn more about his lineage. When the results came back, he shared them with me. It was clear that my sister and I shared only one parent's DNA: our mother's. This confirmed a hunch I'd carried for years that the man I'd always been told was my father was not related to me biologically. I'd sometimes say things like, "If Wayne is really my dad . . . ," but my mom never responded to the openings I'd give her. She kept up the lie.

Once these lab results were in, I called my mom. I was direct with her. I said, "It's clear from these lab results that Wayne isn't my father. Who is?" That's when she finally told me the truth. My biological father was a man she'd barely known, someone she said "sold duck whistles." A man named Phil Robertson.

The years *Duck Dynasty* was on, 2013–2018, I'd been living in Nicaragua, so I was not familiar with the Robertson family. I didn't have any real preconceived notions about them. If we had been following the show at all, things might have been different. But as Jase later pointed out, God had determined beforehand where we would be and when, because he had a plan (Acts 17:26). As it was, neither Tony nor I really knew much about *Duck Dynasty*, and so we didn't feel a sense of being starstruck at all. After I found out Phil was famous, however, I became very selective and didn't talk to anyone else about this outside of our family.

God had determined beforehand where we would be and when, because he had a plan (Acts 17:26).

I was clueless about the show, but my sister had been in the States during *Duck Dynasty* days. So when I told her what our mom said, she knew right away who I was talking about. She knew all the names of the family members who'd been on the show. She told me the oldest son, Al, was a preacher at White's Ferry Road Church in West Monroe, Louisiana, which gave me a little hope. Maybe we had something in common beyond genes. I had an idea. What if I sent a letter in care of the church to Al, laying out what our DNA test results had said and what my mom had told me?

For me, church has always been a safe place. This felt like a good next step. So I looked up the church online. That's when I saw that my father was scheduled to speak there at the end of the year. Tony and I immediately decided to drive down from Missouri to hear him talk. We might never get such a chance again.

How could I possibly even imagine what would happen next? I'm a researcher and a planner, so I immediately began to research and prepare. Though there were plenty of good resources about meeting family members for the first time, there seemed to be zero precedent for reaching out to a biological father who happens to be a celebrity.

So I kept praying, asking God to show me the way forward—the way that would please him and bring him glory. I thanked him for the truth at last and asked him for more truth in his timeline. It was important to me from the start not to cause Kay pain, so I asked God to spare her any suffering that might be caused by me. Kay and Phil seemed to have a happy marriage, and it was very important to me that their relationship not suffer because of me. I asked God to make it clear if he wanted me to take a different path. I'd felt like an imposition growing up with my dysfunctional family. The last thing I wanted to do was impose on another family.

Going to hear Phil speak seemed like a good way for me to check him out without disrupting his life. I had a copy of the original letter I'd sent by way of the church and took it with me to the event. I wasn't sure I could go through with personally delivering it, but I wanted to have it available just in case. I suspected I wouldn't be able to string together two coherent words. A letter would have to suffice.

I'm not normally a crier, but that day I shed more than a few tears there in the car in the parking lot. My heart was full of so many emotions welling up from the past—feelings like I didn't belong and that I was unwanted. The devil was trying to whisper in my ear that day, saying things like, *He doesn't want to know you. Who would? You're nothing to him.* As Tony held my hand, I knew I had his love and support, and that gave me courage. Together we got out of the car and went in.

There was a lot of camouflage in the church that day. That was the first thing that struck me. I'd never seen so much camo. Then heads began to turn. I turned, too, and watched as the man I believed to be my father entered the building flanked by a security detail. That was so surreal. It also gave me a sense of how revered Phil is. Hearing him preach, my respect for him grew. A connection and a sense of conviction stirred in me. It gave me the courage to deliver the letter, and after the service ended, I walked up to one of the bearded guys (it was Jase).

I said, "Would you please give this to your dad? It means a lot to me."

He said, "Sure," and tucked it into his bag.

I'd done all I could do. I'd delivered the truth. I felt at peace. It was out of my hands.

In the days and weeks to come, as events unfolded, I continually found myself surrendering the whole process to God. I'm a control freak, in recovery. My preference is to have a plan and contingency plans—and contingencies for any contingencies. But this was so much bigger than me. Very little of it was within my control.

My phone rang. The voice on the other end of the line was Al's cousin, Phil's nephew Zach. He was friendly and kind and said he was calling on behalf of the family, who, understandably, had some questions. As we talked, it was as if the Holy Spirit in me recognized the Holy Spirit in Zach. That gave me such a measure of peace. We agreed to take paternity tests in our respective places before this went any further. This seemed prudent and wise.

A few days later, Zach called me with the results. He said, "Phyllis, it's a match. You're Phil Robertson's long-lost daughter. There's a redemption story here. God is redeeming something. He's making beauty from ashes." Even as he was delivering the life-changing results, he was seasoning it with truth from God's Word. I'll always remember that. It was so helpful, so fortifying. He told me the family was ready to reach out and connect.

I asked, "What about Miss Kay? Is she okay with this?"

Out of everyone, she's the one I had the most concern about. My existence was proof positive of her husband's unfaithfulness years ago. As a wife and mother, I hated the idea of causing her pain. As much as I longed to know my real father, I did not want to disrupt their life together as a couple, and I didn't want to cause Miss Kay, in particular, any discomfort. I didn't want to bring up Phil's past in a bad way. Even though none of it was my fault, I cared deeply about how this might affect her.

Zach said, "Kay is a gracious woman. You'd have to know her and know her story. She wants this too."

Since I had already surrendered this situation to the Lord, and I recognized the Holy Spirit in Zach, I trusted him at his word. We agreed to set up a meeting in West Monroe. They invited me, Tony, and our two sons and their fiancées to their home.

As that call ended, I felt so many things at once. I felt hopeful, scared, excited. I breathed a prayer of thanks.

It wasn't long before Al, Jase, Willie, and Jep began to send me texts. They seemed as excited to meet me as I was them. Then Al and Lisa volunteered to meet us at the airport on February 21, 2020, and drive us to meet my father and Miss Kay at their house. After forty-five years, I was finally going to meet my real father.

I'm a very private person. I had no intention of causing the family undue attention. I think we were pretty successful. But once the guys talked about it on the *Unashamed* podcast, months later, the tabloids jumped on it and added their sensational spin—at least in the headlines. When it came to the actual articles, they quoted family members from the podcast, so they got it right. They were reporting what was actually true.

But up to that point, I was especially careful not to pay attention to media. All my life I've been able to process a lot. I now really needed to filter. The only voices I cared to have in my head were from God and my family.

That flight to Monroe was strange. I had no idea what to think or expect, so I didn't think about anything. I was in the clouds, literally and figuratively.

When I stepped off the airplane, I was looking around for where to go, and the first thing I noticed was my sister-in-law Lisa. She'd been watching for me and found me in the crowd. Something in her eyes was so compassionate and warm that I began to cry. She hugged me so tight. I'm not sure what she said, but I know for sure how it felt. I experienced an immediate sense of belonging.

Lisa was the ideal person to be my first encounter. So much grace. She knows what it feels like to be inside and yet outside, and she has a peace about her. Our meeting could have been awkward, but it wasn't. Not for a minute. We both cried for the first few minutes. Then I introduced her to Tony and the kids. She took us to where Al was outside, waiting with the car. He immediately hugged me and treated me like family. It could have been uncomfortable, but it never was. He was simply the brother I had had for a lifetime and just didn't know it.

On the drive over, Al tried to prepare me. He said, "Phil's not a real hugger like we are. Don't expect him to talk a lot, but he's listening, believe me." Things like that.

When we pulled up, Phil and Kay were in the yard at Al's house. I got out, and Phil walked up and took my face in his hands. The first thing he said was, "I never knew," which was so heartening. It spoke peace to my deepest fears. Because what if he'd known and didn't want to have a relationship with me? He continued to look into my tear-filled eyes. He said, "I'm trying to see if there's any of me in there." Evidently he did. He took hold of my hand, and Kay took hold of the other. Together we went into the house.

I think of that moment a lot. Doesn't it just remind you of God? He wants us to look at him, so he can connect with us. We might run from him and cover up that *imago Dei*. But all he asks is that we turn our faces to him, so we can reflect back his divine love.

Al had cautioned me not to get my hopes up about my dad's ability to be nurturing. Maybe it's because he raised four boys before he knew me, but for whatever reason, Al's experience and mine have been very different. My father is one of the most affectionate people I've ever known. He's sweet, attentive, gentle, nurturing, patient, and loving. He's everything I could ever want in a dad and more. So when he invited us to move next door, we said yes without hesitation. We moved from Missouri six months later in August 2020.

We have a lot of catching up to do.

To know Phil is to know his love for God's creation. He loves hunting, he's a preservationist and a conservationist, and he loves

[God] wants us to look at him, so he can connect with us. We might run from him and cover up that *imago Dei*. But all he asks is that we turn our faces to him, so we can reflect back his divine love.

the land. My whole life I've felt like I didn't quite fit in, and now I feel like the puzzle fits together perfectly. It makes sense, now that I know I'm a daughter of a hunter who's the best in his field.

We hunt, we "brush the blind," we go hiking, or we drive around on his hunting land in a side-by-side. Since we live so close, Dad will sometimes knock on our door at dawn and say, "Let's go see if there are ducks in this one hole." I always say yes. Even if I'm still in my pajamas, I'll grab a coat and go. That's why I'm here. I'm here to get to know my father. And as we get to know each other, we're both growing and changing in unexpected ways.

Not long ago it was Kay's birthday, and the family was having a party for her. I asked Dad about it and found out he wasn't planning to come. I could understand him not wanting to gather for a big party because he's not much of a socializer, but he wasn't even going to get her a present. I said, "Dad, why don't you buy Miss Kay a gift? It would blow her mind if you did. What would her face look like if she opened something you had personally picked out?"

He didn't have a response to that, but I could tell he was thinking it through. So I said, "I could call ahead to your favorite jewelry store and see if they'd let you pick out something while they're closed. That way there'd be nobody else watching."

He said, "We could do that."

My dad hadn't been inside a store for seven years. *Seven years!* But he started thinking about his children and grandchildren. He told me he wanted them to see him respecting and honoring his wife as the Bible commands. He genuinely loves Kay and wants to treat her well. At the same time, he was thinking generationally, about what kind of legacy he's leaving.

We went together to the jewelry store. He picked out a lovely necklace to give Miss Kay. When they handed him the necklace in a gift bag, he turned around and asked, "What do I do now?" The gift bag with tissue paper was as foreign to my outdoorsman dad as a duck call would be to a city slicker. I said, "That's it. There's nothing left for you to do but hand it to her, just as it is." And he did. She was so surprised and delighted. The look on her face brought me great joy.

Looking back, I see that if we hadn't been obedient to what God was doing along the path, if our choices weren't aligned with the Word of God, the redemption of our relationship would not have been possible. When we aren't obedient, it affects not just our lives, but it has a ripple effect on our children, our friends. So many people are affected that we won't even know how many this side of heaven. I just keep learning more and more how important it is to walk in faith. To surrender in faith to God every single day.

Beauty from Ashes

The addition of Phyllis to this family has been surprising in so many ways. She's become a dear sister to me. I lost my own sister and brother years ago to alcoholism. I'm so grateful to God for the gift of a sister I never expected. I've also seen a softening in Phil's roar. It's been amazing.

"It is amazing to see what beauty God can bring out of our messes," he said. "My daughter is a living testimony of that."

Kay sees it too. It's impossible to miss, really. We've all witnessed it in things like Phil's shopping for that special necklace he gave Kay on her birthday at her surprise party. He's never done anything like that before.

All our stories have come together in a beautiful way, as Zach predicted. God has brought beauty from the ashes. God's Spirit working in our individual lives has a generational effect—affecting generations and increasingly larger circles of people. It's glorious! If Kay hadn't followed Christ years ago, Phil could have ended up dead—or worse. Instead, Phil turned his life over to Christ. And because of Al's and my troubles, Al developed a tremendous passion to help families and couples, a passion he didn't have before. I deeply regret having broken Al's heart, but I know that as a couple, if we hadn't been redeemed, the reunion between Phyllis and Phil might never have happened.

These days we have Tony and Phyllis at our house once a week for a meal. That's been a good way to connect on a different level. They've been intentional to make space in their hearts and lives for us in special ways too, like when Al officiated their son's wedding.

I Always Wanted a Daughter

When we found out Phil had a daughter he didn't know about, I never had any thought other than accepting her into the family. It didn't surprise me at all, really. God had been preparing my heart for it, I guess. Besides, when you love somebody the way I love Phil, you love their kid like they're your own. At least that's the way I see it. Still, there is one thing that got my goat. The other day, I said, "Phil, I'm still mad about one thing."

He looked at me and asked, "What?"

I said, "I always wanted a girl. Now I finally get one, but she's forty-five, and I can't play dolls or any of that fun stuff. I missed all that."

Phyllis heard that, and she said, "Really? My mom didn't do any of that, Kay. I want to do it now!"

So we're planning to go shopping soon.

In a way, I always knew. I knew Phil was running around with other women during those wild years, and I didn't want the boys to be shocked when they found out later. The way I imagined it, some boy would come along one day and say Phil was his daddy. Many times I said to our boys, even when they were very young, "Some boy is gonna come along and say, 'Your dad is my dad.'" That might sound weird, but I wanted them to be prepared. And since Phil had only fathered boys, it didn't occur to me that he could have a girl. I think that prepared them some, but mostly God did the preparing.

It's been interesting how intentional Al has been with his sister. He was always the nurturer of my boys, almost like a dad to the others when Phil was living his wild days. But God has prepared his heart in other ways too. If Lisa and Al hadn't handed over their relationship to God to redeem years ago—who knows what would have happened with Phyllis? Lisa and Al have played a vital role in helping Phyllis feel welcomed into this family. They're very close to Phyllis and Tony and their kids.

How would that have happened otherwise? God was working all the time, as usual.

Welcome or Not

It's true that God prepared me to help welcome Phyllis into the family. When I first saw her, I hugged her. I said, "Listen, you don't have to hug everybody you meet today. I do want you to hug me, though." Touch is my love language, and I wanted her to know I love her. I wanted to communicate that I am a safe place for her. Phyllis is not a big hugger, but I have hugged her every time I've seen her since. She's gotten used to it and even kind of likes it now, I think.

I think she felt a bit like an outsider when she first got here, and I related to that. The family viewed me with distrust for quite a long while after I broke Al's heart all those years ago. It took a lot of work to rebuild our relationships. It was important to me to make amends, and I did. But I'll never forget what it felt like to be outside their circle even when I was officially part of it.

Since I related to that outsider position, I instantly connected with Phyllis. She is a member of the family by blood, and yet for forty-five years she was a stranger. What started as a seed of compassion grew in the days and months that followed. I witnessed her heart and her humor and decided we would not just be family; we'd also be friends.

That kind of empathy can be a great starting place for a relationship. It's much easier to relate to someone who's struggling when you've experienced similar pain or grief or shame. As much as it pained us at the time, that point of connection can help us welcome others into a relationship. And that can make all the difference.

Phyllis felt like an imposition for too much of her life. That's awful. It grieves God's heart. And yet so many of us feel that way: unwelcome. Well, no more. Phyllis's earthly father and his family have welcomed her with open arms. And I pray that God gets every bit of the glory.

I sense God turning my past experiences into something he can use for his glory in other ways too. Those of us who've been down a difficult road—even if it was years ago—aren't just more empathetic; we're also less likely to judge. Compassion bubbles up in me at the most unexpected moments.

Recently I heard Phil say he has no memory of Phyllis's mom telling him she was pregnant, even though she says she did at the time. I said, "Phil, I get it. There are pieces of my life that I just can't recall because I was out of it. I did what you did. When I wasn't living for the Lord, I was often drunk or high. I understand how it feels to search your brain and come up completely empty."

It's hard to believe that about both of us now, but it's a fact. Our salvation story is a part of who we were and part of who we are today. God kindly gave us each other "for such a time as this" (Esther 4:14). When shame threatens to engulf us, we're there for each other, and we can remind each other of God's mercy and grace.

Phyllis's story reminds me always to choose God's way. He has many blessings to give—our part is just choosing to

With a surrendered heart, God can do anything. It's the surrender that invites his miracles.

surrender. Phyllis came into this situation with such a heart for God. She was always mindful of how her news was going to affect Phil and Miss Kay. I can understand her being anxious. She had plenty of reasons to be nervous. Now, though, she sees how God was working at every stage, orchestrating their reunion. What God was up to was nothing short of redemption. He wanted to bless her beyond anything she could imagine.

If Phyllis had not given God control over her life, this whole story would have gone quite differently. Tony, too, had given God control, and that made a huge difference. With a surrendered heart, God can do anything. It's the surrender that invites his miracles.

Your Turn

- What lies or secrets have disrupted your life? How did they affect you and those you love?
- What has surrendering to God looked like in your life?
- Has God ever answered your prayers in unexpected ways, as he did Kay's prayer for a daughter? What did that look like?
- Has God redeemed a broken relationship in your life? How did that play out?
- Do you have any relationships in your life right now that need to be redeemed?

Prayer: *God, you've given me a story. Would you give me the courage to share it?*

4

Look Who's Talking

Taking Captive the Thoughts in Your Head

Those who look to him are radiant;
their faces are never covered with shame.

PSALM 34:5

If you saw me before I surrendered my life to Jesus, you wouldn't recognize me.

The old me used to dress to be noticed. I wanted men to stop and look. The shorter the dresses and shorts the better. I went for lower necklines to show off my curves and wore lots of makeup. I went to the tanning bed year-round. I carried myself as if to say, "I'm available."

I wanted to be provocative. You've seen the way prostitutes dress, the way their clothes invite the idea of sex. Satan was whispering to me the same thing he whispers to them: *The only thing you're good for is sex. If you don't please men who want you for their carnal pleasure, you're worthless.* I believed him.

The soundtrack to my life was music about sex, having sex, being sexy, having sex in the back of a car, and so on. I migrated toward songs that reflected the things Satan was whispering in my head all day: *You're dirty and used up. Sex appeal is your only power.*

Alan and I had started dating when neither of us was following the Lord. We broke up for a time and then got back together. Phil knew about our past, so he told Alan, "Either convert her or cull her." He wanted to make sure Al married a Christian. In all honesty, I was desperate to marry Al. I would have done anything for him. In my mind, he'd been my knight in shining armor since I first saw him when I was just a girl in sixth grade. So I let myself be "converted." In my heart, though, I never really accepted Jesus as Lord. I did, however, regularly attend church service. And once Al decided to become a pastor, I became a reluctant pastor's wife. My heart was not in it. I did not care to sing along with the songs at worship. The lyrics didn't ring true. I felt like a liar when I tried to join in.

What felt real to me was the music I listened to. Songs about sex, longing, and secret affairs. The louder the music, the better. I rocked out to music and consumed other media that normalized the notion that sex was a game, a secret, or a weapon. Those words drowned out the truth that said I was worth more. Instead, I agreed with the lies and kept turning up the volume on the noise.

I loved my husband. I loved him more than I loved myself. However, I did not believe he loved me. I believed I was useful to him but not for abiding love. That is why, during all those years, I never turned him down. I believed the only thing I was good for was a man's pleasure. My lot in life was simply to be used by men. I was often stressed and nervous, and I knew I was not being authentic. On the outside I was brash and bold, but inside I felt broken. I was not whole. I carried a secret shame.

I spent a lot of time at my grandmother's house growing up. That's where the abuse by a relative started when I was young, around age seven. I remember that once I tried to tell my mother but was unable to. She insisted I stay in this unsafe place where I would often encounter the man who stole my innocence and used me for his own immoral purposes. I kept this horrible secret for more than a decade. I finally worked up the courage to resist him when he approached me at a family funeral. Maybe it was the venue, but whatever the case, I told him if he didn't stop I'd tell my father. We both knew my father would have killed him if I did. After that, he left me alone. But the damage had been done. I'd swallowed the lie that I was damaged goods, used up. My worth was only in my sexual appeal. Any value I had was dependent on my ability to provide men sexual pleasure.

Between keeping this toxic secret and all the lies I'd crafted to avoid the truth, I was in constant turmoil. Peace with God or myself was inconceivable to me.

The Truth Is Out

We'd been married for about fifteen years when Alan discovered I'd been lying to him about a lot of things. The evidence seemed to point to an affair. He'd known something was wrong; he just hadn't been able to pinpoint what it was. He had to know the truth. Finally, after hours of arguing and my denying everything, I finally gave up and told the truth: I'd been having a sexual affair for fourteen months. Al was devastated but relieved to know that he wasn't crazy. When I finally said the words aloud, something inside me completely broke. I'd been lying for so long. What would become of me now that I was fully exposed?

I'll never forget lying facedown in our backyard, crying out to God in desperation, physically spent from hours of emotional turmoil and coming face-to-face with reality. I had come to the end of myself.

In God's infinite mercy, he met me there. Immediately I

[God] embraced me as his prodigal child, and it was as if I'd been wrapped in light, even as I continued to soak the ground with my tears.

felt a lightening. I felt a presence. It was the Spirit of the Lord. He embraced me as his prodigal child, and it was as if I'd been wrapped in light, even as I continued to soak the ground with my tears.

As I sobbed, I felt God whispering how much he loved me and how beautiful I was in spirit, and how my value was worth the ultimate sacrifice: his life! He would have died on the cross just for me if necessary. He'd suffered excruciating pain just for me, in the broken condition I came to him in. Hearing those words over and over, I began to realize, *This is reality. This is truth.* I believed him.

Once I knew how much I was loved and valued by my heavenly Father, I began to change. When I became a true Jesus follower and started my journey to freedom from my past, I was radical about it. This was no surface cleanup. It was Extreme Makeover: Lisa Robertson edition.

That was what I wanted. I *wanted* to reflect the image of God. I wanted my outward appearance to reflect my change of heart. I'd confessed my sins and been forgiven, so I felt clean all the way down into my soul. I never wanted to feel the effects of sin again. I wanted my inside and outside to match.

> [Contemplating] the Lord's glory, [we] are being *transformed* into his image with ever-increasing glory, which comes from the Lord, who is the Spirit." (2 Corinthians 3:18, emphasis added)

When my heart changed, my countenance changed. The dark makeup and tanned skin were no longer necessary. Why would a saved daughter of the King hide her face?

That cheap look didn't suit me at all anymore. I gave away things that were too tight. I threw out skirts, dresses, and shorts that were too short. Low-cut tops. Gone. Christ died for *me*! He left the ninety-nine to search for *me*! And now I was found by him. He'd pulled me close, and I wanted to stay close. I was in a place of deep need for Jesus, and I was careful to stay close to him.

A counselor was helping me. Al and I were separated, and I wanted help with addressing the deep wounds that had contributed to my lack of self-worth and betrayal of Al. This counselor asked me to pretend a certain person was sitting in an empty chair during sessions in her office. She'd then coach me, helping me say what I needed to say to that person. It seemed silly at first, but then once I did it, I felt so much better. I'd been holding a lot of hurt inside for years. Now that the truth was out, this practice helped me get my voice back. It helped me to say things out loud that I'd been holding in tightly all my life. That's when I started talking to God out loud.

At first this felt strange, crazy even, but soon I realized how helpful it was. When I talked to God, I felt heard, connected, and loved. It became a daily practice for me to talk to God when I was in the car on my way to and from work. One day I got into the car and the radio was on. I started praying, talking to God about this and that, and then I noticed the song playing on the radio. The lyrics were about "making love," but it was like sex was dirty and meant nothing. I knew God wouldn't approve of that, so I shut it off.

The next day I heard just the first few notes of a song that had been a favorite of mine for many years. The music made me shudder. It triggered strong negative and hurtful feelings. My taste in music had changed. I could no longer belt out those songs of sexual fantasies or about lying, cheating hearts. How could I have once thought those songs were good? Their implied promises were empty! The ideas that the "right" man could complete me and that sex could satisfy my every longing were a lie. Hollow. There was nothing any man could offer that my heavenly Father could not provide! I'd never noticed how toxic the words were. I had been listening to them for too long. Now that I knew they'd been poisoning me, I spit them out.

Talking with God had alerted me to how I'd been letting in words and thoughts that were harmful. Lying voices had infiltrated my thinking with my consent.

God was nudging me to listen more closely to determine what was true and what was a lie. I sensed his gentle voice speaking to me often. He'd nudge me in the gentlest way to change the station, literally and figuratively. *Talk to me instead, Lisa*, he would say. *Listen to my truth.* He pursued me. He wanted our interaction as much as I needed it.

A verse I'd read in the Psalms came to me then:

> As a deer longs for streams of water,
> so I long for You, God.
> I thirst for God, the living God.
> (Psalm 42:1–2 HCSB)

Staying in tune with my Father's loving voice was my heart's desire. My heart responded to songs about grace, love, and forgiveness. Hearing their words, my spirit responded, recognizing

[God is] a
friend as well
as the source
of my salvation
and strength.
He's always
ready to talk.

his voice of truth. I'd been given a new song! "Sing to the LORD a new song; sing to the LORD, all the earth" (Psalm 96:1).

Drive time wasn't the only time I wanted to sing and talk to God. I could sing praises anytime. I could talk to God anytime too. In fact, all the time. With prayer, I could hear from him and be reminded that he had never left me. He hadn't left when I was abused as a girl. He was there and his heart had broken for me too. He hadn't forsaken me. And even though the consequences of my own sin threatened to undo all that I held dear—my relationship with Alan and my family—God was with me, arms wide open, ready and willing to redeem me. To save me.

This habit of communicating with God became a life habit I still hold to. I talk to God all the time. He's a friend as well as the source of my salvation and strength. He's always ready to talk. That might sound intimidating, and believe me, I get it. He is Lord of the universe as well as our Father. As intimidating as it may be, I do it anyway. It's surprising how easy he is to talk to!

Voices of Encouragement

The week after Alan asked me to leave our home, I went to church. I made my way to the front after the worship service ended. One of the church leaders read aloud a letter I'd written to the church. It was one of the hardest things I've ever done, but I did it. The Bible said, "Confess your sins to each other" (James 5:16), so I wanted to do exactly that. I made a full confession in front of all the people I'd lied to for years and asked for their forgiveness.

My walk reflected the way I'd changed. I changed so much that many people did not even recognize me. About six months into my recovery, an older man at church stopped me and shook my hand and said I had never looked better. His exact words were that I "glowed with the Spirit of the Lord." Such a compliment would have made me uncomfortable when I didn't want to be seen as anything other than an object of sexual appeal. Now it was sweet music to my ears. I never would have believed that an observation from someone about my appearance could bring me such joy.

Transformation is hard. It was probably one of the hardest things I've ever done. It was also one of the most rewarding. In my old life, I never could have imagined that someone would say they saw the Spirit of the Lord shining through me.

Not everyone was quick to forgive and trust me again, though, which I totally understood and respected. My church family supported me in an amazing way during this season. Jesus alone had saved me from my sin, but I needed practical help. I'd lost everything. Getting back on my feet was a monumental task. I could not have done it on my own.

Strength Through Sisterhood

My sisters in Christ became a lifeline to me, especially during the weeks and months following Alan's discovery of my affairs. My best friend, Paula, had suspected that something was amiss.

She had even asked me point-blank if I was having an affair. I'd denied anything was going on. I'd lied to her like I'd lied to everyone I cared about, even myself. When I confessed what I'd done and handed my life over to Jesus, Paula prayed with me.

I knew I needed to study God's Word. I was hungry to know what it said and how it applied to me. I wasn't sure I really grasped what the gospel was and what it meant for me. Paula invited a handful of women to talk with me and study God's Word with us. Laura, Lynne, Natalie, and Kim were the first to help me study the Bible. My eyes were finally open, and I was hungry to know and accept the words of Jesus. I was in a state of wonder. How had God's peace and love been available to me all this time and I'd missed it? These dear women helped usher me into a fuller experience of his love, providing a true example of the value and strength found in sisterhood.

Laura was single, so she invited me to stay with her until I figured out what was next. At least three nights each week a group of us would study and talk and cry together. I trusted them with my full confession. We don't talk a lot about confession these days. What a mistake that is!

Confessing is hard but necessary. We have to acknowledge the helpless position our sin puts us in, so we are able to receive the ultimate truth: Jesus' saving grace. As hard as it was, unburdening myself of the truth about the sin I'd been carrying around for far too long came as a relief. These dear friends reminded me that Jesus cast my sins away, as far as the east is from the west (Psalm 103:12). Truth himself forgave me. Redeemed me. I could feel my roar growing inside, getting ready to join my voice with my sisters' voices.

Truth himself forgave me. Redeemed me. I could feel my roar growing inside, getting ready to join my voice with my sisters' voices.

After a couple of weeks, I announced, "I'm ready to make Jesus the Lord of my life." Kim's house had a pool, so Paula baptized me right there in her swimming pool. What a special event that was! I knew then I would be okay, even if Al and I didn't reconcile. I'd been really and truly saved. I had the Holy Spirit, and I knew I could make it, especially with these sisters in Christ surrounding me and helping me.

Even though I felt better inside than I ever had, I'd lost everything to get to that place.

I didn't have a job at Duck Commander anymore, so Paula helped me find another job. She lived across the street from the house I'd shared with Al and let me stay with her so I could go and take care of my girls without being in Alan's space. For several weeks he didn't have much to do with me. He'd speak to me only in yes-or-no answers.

Al worked at the church, and one day some of the leaders came to him and said, "Here's what we think needs to happen. Lisa should go into a recovery program, and y'all need to not see each other for a year to see how it goes." They were prescribing quite a few stipulations in order for our marriage to be reconciled.

Al told them, "Out of respect, I'd ask that you back off."

Later Al called me and asked if I'd meet with him. My heart dropped. I honestly thought he was going to hand me divorce papers. Instead, he told me about his meeting with those men. He said, "Lisa, this is our marriage, not theirs. They're overstepping. I want to try to see if we can make a go of this. I don't want to be away from you for a year. I wanted to talk with you about this. What do you think?"

I couldn't believe he called me for my opinion about one of the most important decisions of his life. Even though I was the person who'd hurt him the worst, he called *me.* His peers were trying to protect him from me, and I completely understood where they were coming from and said so. During that conversation, we both realized we wanted to make our marriage work.

I had confessed my sin, and my heart was surrendered to the Lord. Al could see that I'd changed. It was a radical change—the way I dressed, the way I talked, the way I interacted with men, the music I listened to, the way I carried myself. My whole disposition had changed. But I hadn't done it for Al. I had done it because at last I knew my own need for Jesus, who is Truth.

I love how God draws us into relationship with him. As an extension of this grace, God gives us community. He gives us brothers and sisters to help us on our journey. The moment we say yes to him, we're part of a family. I never appreciated this aspect of salvation until I experienced it for myself. I didn't know what I was missing until I found it. Now I can't imagine life without it!

I've been friends ever since with the women who helped me through that deeply painful and yet beautiful part of my life. I'm especially grateful to Paula, who held my feet to the fire and challenged me to be the best version of me I could be. We've seen each other through a lot in the years since. I don't know that I'd have made it otherwise. Thank God, I will never have to find out. And you don't have to either!

The closer you get to God, the closer you get to his family of believers. And the more you know of his goodness, the greater

When you've been healed of something, that's God's victory. You can't keep it to yourself. You need to roar. Your own unique roar! And it's even more powerful when you join your roar with the collective roar found in true sisterhood.

your personal influence and encouragement will be. You become an extension of his glory. After all, when you've been healed of something, that's God's victory. You can't keep it to yourself. You need to roar. Your own unique roar! And it's even more powerful when you join your roar with the collective roar found in true sisterhood.

The women who surrounded me and prayed with me in my darkest hour are still very dear to me. We've now been there for each other for more than twenty years. Our lives haven't been all rosy. We've faced infertility, adoption, divorce, births, deaths, and other challenges—but we've had each other to pray with. To laugh with. To cry with. To love with. And that, to me, gives glory to God. None of these things would have happened if they hadn't been there for me, walked that path with me. Life's journey isn't always easy and pretty. Sometimes it's dark and painful. But it's so much better when you have someone to walk with you.

Kay's Takeaways

When I hear Lisa's story, I'm reminded that nothing is impossible with God. I'll never forget the night Lisa finally came clean about her sin. Al came to our house and told Phil and me what had happened. I had never seen him so low. His heart was broken into a thousand pieces. Seeing him like that was so hard. Al was a little boy when Phil was running with the devil, and he was an incredible help to me back then. He'd practically raised his brothers, and he was so mature and helpful. For that reason, Alan will always hold a special place in my heart. I didn't want anyone or anything to hurt him ever again. After he came to us that night, I planned never to let Lisa back into my heart or my family.

But in the days and weeks that followed, the changes in Lisa's life blew me away. I hardly recognized her. She wrote each of us in the family a letter, confessing what she'd done, apologizing for the hurts she'd caused, and making her intentions clear. Then Al really and truly forgave her. And I forgave her too. Her life change had been dramatic.

I'm proud to say that Lisa has become one of my dearest friends. I can't imagine life without her. We enjoy sisterhood that goes way beyond earthly family.

Isn't that just like God? To take a situation so messed up, so marked by trauma, lies, betrayal, and corruption, and redeem every bit of it? Al and Lisa's relationship was radically redeemed. People in the church saw the transformation and asked them to take on premarital counseling. Then to help out at marriage retreats. Then to do one-on-one marriage counseling. Their impact grew and grew. Now the two of them speak all over the country. They're not teaching some self-help methodology either. They're simply sharing their story and pointing people to Jesus.

The other thing I noticed is how Lisa's close friendships started with an intimate confession. We have to acknowledge our sin with God—even though he knows everything. Our confession is not for his benefit; it's for our own. It's when we bring what's hidden out into the light that the healing begins. What a gift!

Conflicting Voices

Once the truth was out, I realized that the voices in my head can't always be trusted. They can be whispers—or even shouts—from the devil himself. And, as Scripture tells us, the devil is like a prowling lion, "looking for someone to devour" (1 Peter 5:8). He's hunting, and his aim is to take us out! He's also called the "accuser," because what he says about us is mean, hateful, and unkind (Revelation 12:10). Believing what he says can be ruinous. He is the father of lies (John 8:44).

God's voice is never accusing. It's always gentle, firm, sure—and true.

Remember when I said the first few notes of a song could make me feel a certain way? These days, if I'm feeling uneasy, I tune in to listen carefully to what's going on in my head. Scripture refers to this as "taking every thought captive" (2 Corinthians 10:5 HCSB). Essentially, I ask myself, *What is going on in my head right now? What are the voices saying? Are they accurate? Are they accusing? Or are they speaking truth?*

Often the source of my uneasiness is a thought of doubt or worry. Fears about health, finances, relationships, career, or loved ones fill me with anxiety. The thoughts sound like:

I worry that . . .
I don't think I can . . .
What if . . .

Scripture tells us that God's perfect love casts out all fear (1 John 4:18). That casting out of all fear happens when we *acknowledge* the fear. So paying attention to our specific fears is the first step. We need to capture them and hold them up to the light. We know God gave us his Word for our instruction and encouragement, so we should evaluate the accuracy of those thoughts in our heads (Romans 12:2, 15:4). What does Scripture say? What does it say about me? About God? Then we speak back God's Word over that troubling thought. The Holy Spirit is especially helpful with doing this (John 14:26).

I worry that . . .

Lord, in your Word you comfort me with these words: "Do not be afraid, for I have ransomed you. I have called you by name; you are mine. When you go through deep waters, I will be with you. When you go through rivers of difficulty, you will not drown. When you walk through the fire of oppression, you will not be burned up; the flames will not consume you" (Isaiah 43:1–2 NLT). *Take away my worry, Lord God.*

I don't think I can . . .

Lord, fortify me with your Spirit and the promise of your Word: "For God has not given us a spirit of fear and timidity, but of power, love, and self-discipline" (2 Timothy 1:7 NLT).

What if . . .

Lord, any number of things can happen, but your Word never fails. You promised, "I will never leave you nor forsake you." So we may boldly say, "The Lord is my helper; I will not fear. What can man do to me?" (Hebrews 13:5–6 NKJV).

Finally, simply speaking Jesus' name ushers in peace. His name causes demons to quake (James 2:19)—they fear his power (Mark 5:7). Satan is the father of lies (John 8:44), and lies cannot exist in the presence of Jesus, who is Truth (John 14:6)! The presence of ultimate Truth dispels fear and quiets the storms inside.

Returning to the strength of true sisterhood, I find that it is helpful to stay honest about what's going on in my life with my sisters in Christ. Letting one another know what we're praying about keeps us accountable. And it has the added benefit of helping us notice when our prayers get answered, because then we can rejoice together! I know my friends are always willing to pray for and with me too. That's a wonderful gift. I think back over the years about all the things my friends and I have seen each other through, and I rejoice, remembering that we're all in this together. And we know it's important to use our voices to bring God the glory he deserves.

Miriam's Sister Roar

When I think about women using their voices to proclaim the glory of God, I think of Miriam. She was Moses' sister. In fact, she was his big sister, the one who watched him from afar when their mother, Jochebed, put Moses in a tar-covered basket and set him afloat at the edge of the Nile River because the Egyptian king had demanded that all Hebrew baby boys be killed.

Can you imagine? What a place to put an infant! If it seems like Jochebed was taking a big risk by putting her baby in such a strange place, you have to remember that it was amazing he'd lived that long in the first place.

> But when [Jochebed] could no longer hide him, she took an ark of bulrushes for him, daubed it with asphalt and pitch, put the child in it, and laid it in the reeds by the river's bank. And his sister stood afar off, to know what would be done to him. (Exodus 2:3–4 NKJV)

At the time, the Israelite population—God's people—were being fruitful and multiplying, even under the tyranny of the Egyptian king, and he worried that they would grow in numbers and rise up against him. But he needed their labor to build his empire, so he tried hard to keep them under his control by keeping their population down. He'd commanded the Israelite midwives to murder any newborn boy babies. However, the midwives protested that the hardy Israelite women gave birth before they could get there to do their job.

Notice a theme here? Daughters of God were undermining the evil schemes of the pharaoh!

Back to Miriam. She watched over her baby brother floating among the reeds. Scripture doesn't tell us much, but we know she kept herself hidden. Imagine her excitement and even fear when she saw the pharaoh's daughter approaching. That was probably pretty intimidating, especially for a young slave girl actively rebelling against the pharaoh! The princess had come to the river with her ladies-in-waiting to bathe. When she saw the baby, she had compassion on him. Miriam saw her chance. She courageously stepped forward and spoke humbly as she offered help. I love the fact that such a young girl had that much courage, wisdom, and savvy!

> Then the daughter of Pharaoh came down to bathe at the river. And her maidens walked along the riverside; and when she saw the ark among the reeds, she sent her maid to get it. And when she opened it, she saw the child, and behold, the baby wept. So she had compassion on him, and said, "This is one of the Hebrews' children."
>
> Then his sister said to Pharaoh's daughter, "Shall I go and call a nurse for you from the Hebrew women, that she may nurse the child for you?" (Exodus 2:5–7 NKJV)

We don't hear much about Miriam for a while because Scripture focuses on Moses for several chapters, telling how he grew up and moved into the house of royalty and privilege after having been nurtured by his Israelite mother and her faith. When Moses saw firsthand how God's people were being wronged, having witnessed the beating of an Israelite slave, he acted out of passion, killing the overseer. Having been spared from death twice as an infant, he now killed someone in the name of justice. Moses fled town in a hurry after that.

> Now it came to pass in those days, when Moses was grown, that he went out to his brethren and looked at their burdens.

> And he saw an Egyptian beating a Hebrew, one of his brethren. So he looked this way and that way, and when he saw no one, he killed the Egyptian and hid him in the sand. And when he went out the second day, behold, two Hebrew men were fighting, and he said to the one who did the wrong, "Why are you striking your companion?"
>
> Then he said, "Who made you a prince and a judge over us? Do you intend to kill me as you killed the Egyptian?"
>
> So Moses feared and said, "Surely this thing is known!" When Pharaoh heard of this matter, he sought to kill Moses. But Moses fled from the face of Pharaoh and dwelt in the land of Midian; and he sat down by a well. (Exodus 2:11–15 NKJV)

Fast-forward to Moses in the desert, with nobody looking out for him any longer. He got work as a shepherd for his father-in-law. He was looking after the sheep when he heard directly from God, who told him to go back to Egypt to tell Pharaoh to release God's people. Moses did, but Pharaoh refused. So God sent plagues on the Egyptians. Ultimately, the thing that convinced Pharaoh to let God's people go was this: God did to the Egyptians what Pharaoh did to the Israelites—he took their firstborn sons, including Pharaoh's. That broke him. "Go!" Pharaoh said. But he quickly changed his mind.

Just when it seemed Moses and the Israelites would be overtaken by Pharaoh's army, the waters of the Red Sea rolled back to allow the Israelites to pass through. Moses, who'd been drawn out of the water as an infant, passed right through the waters of the sea and onto the other side. His life had come full circle in a way.

> For the horses of Pharaoh went with his chariots and his horsemen into the sea, and the LORD brought back the waters of the sea upon them. But the children of Israel went on dry land in the midst of the sea.
>
> Then Miriam the prophetess, the sister of Aaron, took the timbrel in her hand; and all the women went out after her with timbrels and with dances. And Miriam answered them:
>
> "Sing to the LORD,
> For He has triumphed gloriously!
> The horse and its rider
> He has thrown into the sea!" (Exodus 15:19–21 NKJV)

This is where we see Miriam again. The whole of Israel was astounded and grateful for the Lord's deliverance. Miriam led the women of Israel in songs of praise, dancing with a tambourine! It's clear here that the young girl who helped save her brother's life grew up in the tyranny of Egypt without him, but on the other side of the Red Sea found herself reunited with him and, by God's grace, delivered from bondage. She responded naturally, with joy and praise!

Do you love to sing as much as I do? I don't have the gift for it like my sister-in-law Missy, but I do enjoy singing praises when someone like Missy—or Miriam—is leading. The praise of a sister brings me special joy. Anytime we praise, it's a pouring out of gratitude. It's a way of directing our attention to God. We give God the credit for what's good. After all, he's the giver of all good things!

I like to remember that Miriam's sister roar began when she waited quietly and hopefully and then stepped forward with courage and used her voice. That voice developed into a song of praise so strong that we hear it echoing even now, thousands of years later, in the words of Scripture.

If you want to give your own voice a boost of hope, I encourage you to go back and read Miriam's story in its entirety for yourself.

Your Turn

- The radio isn't the only source of "voices." The music, books, podcasts, and shows we let into our minds matter. Do the voices you're listening to jibe with God's truth?
- Are you reaching for your phone first thing in the morning and filling your head with chatter? It helps to keep that phone away and instead wake up and spend time with God, reading his Word and praying quietly, before diving into your day. How do you need to change your morning routine?
- What about social media? Are you "following" people whose voices help you walk in truth, or are you peeking into windows of lives you should probably steer clear of?
- It also helps if you don't book your day so full that you're in such a rush you hurry past folks who might need eye contact and a bit of conversation. How can you make your schedule more flexible?

- It's important not to stare at your phone when someone speaks to you, so that you don't miss an opportunity to connect with them. What can you do to make sure others have your full attention?

5

The Power of Connection

Relationships Make the Difference

Be good friends who love deeply.

ROMANS 12:10 THE MESSAGE

I love how Lisa's friends spoke God's truth to her, don't you? Since she surrendered her heart to Jesus, I've watched her act as a source of God's mercy and grace to those same friends for twenty-plus years. She has prayed with them and supported them through good times and bad. Her presence and words bring comfort to them in real time—and even when she's not around them, she brings them comfort because she's sharing Jesus, who is the ultimate Truth and Life. What an impact!

My Nanny had that kind of impact on me. I'm so grateful for her quiet roar and loving presence in my life. My parents spent a lot of time at the store, working from dawn until late at night, so I spent a lot of time with her. When I close my eyes, I can be right back there with her, shelling peas from her garden and shucking corn. I can hear the sound of her porch swing swaying as she handed out wisdom and love. She always let me know that I was special. That I was known and seen.

Nanny taught me to cook. I wanted to be just like her because she was such a light in my life. My dream was to be the best wife and mother I could be. I had a big imagination, and I had it all planned out. I had all these big ideas about how my life would look. I always dreamed of marrying a pioneer man, and one day I told her I'd found that man in Phil. Even as a teenager he was that way.

Nanny taught me, "One man and one wife for one life." She

told me many times that I'd have to fight for my marriage. I didn't understand that. I thought it was silly because all I wanted was to be the best wife and mother I could be. What man wouldn't want a woman like that? Why would I ever need to fight? She didn't ever fight. I'd watch her and my grandfather. I remember them sitting in their rocking chairs next to that old space heater, holding hands. Nanny would read the Bible out loud to him. I thought, *That's what I want.*

Later, when things were bad with Phil, I'd think about Nanny and remember the things she'd said to me and the values she'd taught me. I'd go back in my mind to the times we'd sit together in the swing at her house and recall her saying, "You'll have to fight for your marriage." In my heart, I knew she loved me and wanted the best for me, so I stuck with her advice.

Her faith—not my own—sustained me for a lot of years. I tried to be the best wife and mother I could. But it became more and more impossible for me to do that. I finally came to the end of myself and reached out to God for help. I needed my own faith, my own relationship with the Lord.

What if Nanny hadn't instilled in me that deep desire to be a good wife and mother? What if she hadn't taught me that I'd have to fight for my marriage and family? Her positive voice for good in my life had tremendous impact—kingdom impact. Her quiet roar echoes into eternity!

Unlike Miss Kay, many of us grew up without women of character guiding and nurturing us. I loved my mom, but we did not have a close relationship. I loved my grandmother, but her house was not a safe place for me. So I don't relate to those warm, fuzzy feelings. What a shame that is too. The older generation used to be considered wise. People looked to the elder generation for stability and leadership, for examples of virtue and character. Now that's more the exception than the rule. With the prevalence of drug and alcohol abuse, for instance, it's not safe to assume the "grown-ups"—older women—have the sense or space to listen and offer sound advice to the younger women.

A lot has changed since Nanny sat on the swing listening to Kay dream about the boy she'd marry someday. Our populations are more urban than rural.[4] The divorce rate is nearly 50 percent.[5] There's a cultural norm of anti-authority and a sense that our leaders can't be trusted.[6] Drug use is normalized. A staggeringly high rate of infants are born to single mothers.[7] And church attendance is at a record low.[8]

No wonder there's so much pain, dysfunction, and self-medicating going on. Wounded people wound people, as we say in the 12-step recovery program Celebrate Recovery. Instead of taking personal responsibility, a victim mentality says, *My issues are someone else's problem.*

The world gives sketchy advice: Is your marriage in trouble? Leave. Not ready for a family? You have "choices." Your neighbor is parking on your lawn? Sue. And it's super confusing if you're a woman. The trend of "girl power" says girls don't need others to be strong. Be the boss of your own destiny, right?

Stories like mine, Kay's, and Phyllis's are proof that we need each other. We need strong female role models. We need women strong in the Lord to come alongside us. Without a "Nanny" in your life, what's a sister to do?

Maybe you're thinking, *I don't have that many women in my life, young or old. Sure, there are a lot of women around me but not close to me.* I know exactly what that feels like. There was a time when I, too, was surrounded by women yet still felt very alone.

Kay and I share a deep desire to see women participate in a community. When we have a relationship with the Father, that relationship makes authentic relationships with other women possible. Think about my story—when I was living a lie, I was unable to be honest with others. We can't be honest with others if we haven't been honest with God, who knows us better than we know ourselves. It's God's nature to know everything. We just have to acknowledge our sins and our need for him. "Confess your sins to each other and pray for each other so that you may be healed" (James 5:16).

That kind of healing is beautiful. That's when we have true authenticity. Another word for it is *integrity*—when all the parts of us are whole and uncorrupted by sin. Once we've handed over our lives to God, he redeems every bit of us. Will we still sin? Yes. This side of heaven, we'll all stumble sometimes. The important part is allowing God to reign in our lives, and to work through our lives to redeem those around us too.

Once we have that vertical relationship with the Father, we're a part of the family of God. That's what his body, the church, is! He gives us each other. His family is different. We're a grateful bunch—people who know what it is to be broken and to be made whole. People who've been lost and are now found. We're here for each other when we fall, for when we encounter trials of any kind. We are "God's very own . . . [who] can

[God] gives us sisters to offer an ear, a word of comfort and wisdom, a helping hand, and a faithful presence. Sisterhood is a beautiful thing.

show others the goodness of God, for he called you out of the darkness into his wonderful light" (1 Peter 2:9 NLT). He gives us sisters to offer an ear, a word of comfort and wisdom, a helping hand, and a faithful presence. Sisterhood is a beautiful thing.

As a part of the family of God, we have sisters. Sisters in the family of God are an anointed, nourishing gift!

Sisters in the faith *pray* for one another. We seek the Lord, individually and collectively. We help each other believe.

We rejoice with one another in good times and mourn together in bad times.

We lend our ears, our hands, our hearts, and our resources. We are family!

Sisters love each other. "By this everyone will know that you are my disciples, if you love one another" (John 13:35). That love is both a mindset and an activity.

Crystal and I met through the Muffin group many years ago. (We'll talk about the Muffins in more detail in the next chapter.) I just love her heart for the Lord. She is an inspiration to me. In addition to being a schoolteacher and coach, Crystal is a single mom. Beautiful, smart, and as determined as the day is long, she could be doing anything she wants and have any man she wants. When I've told her that, she's just said, "I'm not interested in any of that. My job is to get my three children into heaven. That's what I care about." She's a no-nonsense kind of person with the biggest heart in the world.

Crystal's son plays football, and if you didn't already know it, you should know this about me: *I love football.* Ever since I was a teenage girl watching Phil quarterback our high school team, to when he was playing for Louisiana Tech, to watching my beloved Saints play today, I've always been a big football fan. So I was happy to go with Crystal to watch her son play recently. The first thing I noticed that night was that the stands were packed out—with women. It struck me as kind of odd how few men there were.

One boy made a terrific play, so I turned to the lady beside me and asked, "Did you see that?"

She replied, "To be honest with you, Miss Kay, I don't know what's happening on that field. I don't know much about football."

Crystal and I got to talking with the other women in the stands, and we discovered that many of them were grandmothers, like me. The boys' daddies weren't there for one reason or another, so the boys asked their grandmothers to come. That was all well and good, but the grandmothers didn't understand the game. They watched their grandsons move around on the field, but they didn't know anything about what they were doing. It was hard for them to encourage the boys, because they didn't know the game. Crystal and I talked about it, and we decided that we might not be able to get those boys' daddies to come to the games, but we could do something about this.

I went home and found a legal pad. I drew a map of all the players. Phil sat down with me and helped me put down a name for all the players: the Xs and Os. The next week, Crystal and I went to another game. We took out that piece of paper and asked each grandmother, "Now, what position is your grandson?" We found out who their boys were, and together we worked out what was going on and who did what. We were all so proud! We'd figured it out *together*.

Sisters

need each

other's

company,

so we

gather.

While it's a shame those boys' daddies don't come to the games, I know this much: the sisters roaring in the stands knew what was going on, and we were cheering. Loudly! We got a kick out of it, and the boys liked it too.

What started as some grandmothers just watching a game together turned into getting together on a heart-to-heart level. You can be with somebody and not really be with them, you know what I mean? When you get to really experience something with some sisters, that's special.

Sisters *need* each other's company, so we *gather*.

We gather to worship in stadiums, churches, and parks.

We gather in homes for Bible studies, meals, and celebrations.

We gather in restaurants, coffee shops, and backyards where there are pools for baptizing.

You'd be surprised at the places we come up with to gather!

Your Turn

- **Who are the women who influenced you when you were growing up?**
- **What are some of the sage wisdom they shared with you?**
- **Where are some of the places you congregate?**
- **Who might God be appointing for you to cultivate a relationship with?**
- **Pray for God to open your eyes to see the people God puts in your path whom he means for you to serve and to love.**

6

Kay's Muffins

Supporting One Another in Groups

Let us consider how we may spur one another on toward love and good deeds, not giving up meeting together . . . but encouraging one another—and all the more as you see the Day approaching.

HEBREWS 10:24–25

Cinnamon, blueberry, banana nut, cranberry nut, lemon poppyseed. I have yet to meet a muffin I don't like. My favorite is probably my Good Morning muffin. I bake it with carrots, apples, and raisins, so it's like having a salad for breakfast when what you're really enjoying is basically a piece of cake you can eat with your hands. I say that's a win-win.

I was holding a batch of my Good Morning muffins that first day when I drove over to Darlene's Girlfriends Dress Shop. I was there to meet with a little group of women who wanted to talk about life, faith, and following Jesus. Darlene met me at the door and led me back to where a handful of women had gathered, sitting on the floor. After we greeted each other, I looked around. There were clothes hanging on metal rods, price tags on rolls, boxes stacked on the floor. I smiled. It was like a perfect girls clubhouse. I couldn't imagine a better place to meet.

We'd gathered to share, so I told them my own story. I felt it was important for them to know I was going to be honest with them. I said, "I'll go first so you don't have to feel vulnerable."

I told them about how my dad had died when I was fourteen, and that when I first started dating in high school, my mom was dating too. I told them how Phil and I got married so young when we found out I had a baby on the way, and I followed Phil to school at Louisiana Tech. I told them I'd had to grow up quick, raising my boys while he was running around on me, getting wilder and wilder with each passing day. I didn't hold anything back. I told it all, about how he'd kicked me and the boys out when I started following the Lord. Then how Phil turned his life over to Jesus too. Even to me it's a dramatic story. And I'm the one who lived it.

The meeting was all so informal. We didn't have an agenda, and since this was before *Duck Dynasty* days, I wasn't used to public speaking. I hadn't planned for any formal Bible study either. It was just a handful of women getting together in the name of Jesus. I said, "Let's all just agree to be teachable and unoffendable. What do we have to be offended about? God is our defender, so there's no need to be defensive when we've got God on our side."

And that's what we did.

We ate muffins and talked about growing up, about romance, marriage, and men—and what the Bible teaches about those things. I could see these women were hungry for Christian companionship. And I felt that because of my years of experience and my relationship with Jesus, God had brought me to that little dress shop for a reason. He had a purpose for me in that place.

At some point, Darlene had to open her shop. Our time was up, so we agreed to come back and meet again the following Tuesday. The only question was, who would bring the muffins?

The more the merrier, I always say. Our little Muffin group felt that way too, I guess, because they came back the next week with friends. And soon we were spilling out of that dress shop's back room. But God had a contingency plan, as he always does. There were picnic tables behind the shop, and since the weather was good, we moved out there.

I'll never forget the day we began talking about good influences, like my Nanny was for me, and how sometimes the people in our lives help us follow Jesus and other times they're not so helpful. I was challenging the girls to think about the people they might need to lean on and some they might need to limit their association with.

"When I'm with her," one of the girls said, pointing across the table, "I drink too much."

Her friend's eyes got as big as saucers and said, "You're blaming your drinking on me? You're the town drunk!"

The first girl lunged across the table and slaps started flying. It was a mess. I couldn't let them hurt each other, so I jumped up and broke up their fight.

The second girl ran from the picnic table to her truck. I was younger then, so I ran and caught up with her. She had just shut that truck door when I came up and put my hand on the window. She rolled it down with tears in her eyes.

I said, "I know you're mad. You can drive away, and that's fine. But you need to know, when you get home, I'll be pulling up right behind you. We're gonna talk this out."

"All right, Miss Kay," she said. "I'll see you in a few minutes."

I went back to the others at the picnic table. That first girl was upset. She said, "I was just telling the truth, Miss Kay, like you always tell us to."

"I know," I said. "We have to be patient with each other. Just because you're comfortable being honest doesn't mean she's ready yet. Let's love each other where we are and not push. We're here to encourage one another, okay?"

She nodded.

Then I left, followed the other girl home, and we talked. It all worked out. Those two brought more girls, and it just grew from there.

We moved on from the picnic tables to our friend Kim's house. In a few years, we outgrew Kim's house, so we used one of the fellowship rooms at our church. Every time we met, we'd bring muffins and other snacks. Sometimes we'd have a little bit of an organized discussion, but mainly we'd just encourage each other in the Lord for a couple of hours. We'd created a safe place for one another, a place to learn from each other and seek the Lord's will for our lives, a place to find our individual and collective roars, a place of true sisterhood.

My testimony might have gotten the Muffin group started, but I wasn't the only one with a story. God is always working in our lives. It makes me think of the verse in Isaiah where God says, "See, I am doing a new thing! Now it springs up; do you not perceive it?" (Isaiah 43:19).

I was perceiving it, all right! When one of the Muffins told about what was going on in her life and how God was working, I'd point it out. I'd stop her right there. I'd ask, did she see it? Did she see how God was working for her good? To prosper her and not to harm her, as the Bible says? I'd thank God for it right then and there.

It did all our hearts good, I think, to be encouraged by our stories of God at work. It was contagious, in a way, because it got to where the others encouraged one another while I just sat back and watched.

Did we pray together? Yes! We prayed a lot. We started our time together with prayer, and we ended it that way too. We sent up a lot of praise and a lot of petitions. We'd cry together but also laugh till our sides hurt.

There's no question in my mind that our Muffin group was an answer to prayers we'd all sent up. We might not have known it, but we needed *fellowship*, which is just an old-fashioned word for Christian community. Paul wrote about it in his letter to Titus:

> Guide older women into lives of reverence so they end up as neither gossips nor drunks, but models of goodness. By looking at them, the younger women will know how to love their husbands and children, be virtuous and pure, keep a good house, be good wives. (Titus 2:3–5 THE MESSAGE)

I think we underestimate the power of a good influence. So many of us are surrounded at work, school, and home by folks who aren't following Jesus. They don't care, they don't know any better, or, like Phil back in the day, they think Christians just want to ruin their fun. Time with kindred spirits—women doing their best to glorify God and take care of business—lifts us up. That's what the Muffin sisterhood was all about. Lifting each other up and giving God the glory.

Those girls were like my own kids in a way. They'd frequently call me up at the house. We'd talk, and I'd help out where I could. There were nights I'd be sound asleep and one of my boys would come and wake me up, saying, "Wake up! One of your girls is on the phone. She's crying! She needs you. Hurry up!"

It was good for me to have all those girls to love and learn with. I was the oldest, so I had the most life experience, but I

Time with kindred spirits—women doing their best to glorify God and take care of business—lifts us up.

learned a lot from them too. The biggest thing was, in those first few years, I had a lot of maturing to do. I tended to take on all their problems personally. When one of them fell away and started not doing so well, I'd get sad. It was like my own child was suffering. I would go home and cry my eyes out. It felt like my heart was breaking. I hadn't learned yet to surrender the outcome to the Lord. I had to learn that I can only do so much and have to leave the rest in the Lord's hands.

Phil was concerned for me. He said, "Honey, you're gonna have to not get so upset. You will wear yourself out and be no good to anyone." I knew he was right. I had to mature in that. And I did.

When *Duck Dynasty* started, Tuesday mornings were spoken for. I had to be there for the show. That was our work, and it wasn't something I could negotiate. Too many people were depending on me at home. I wasn't free to meet with my Muffins anymore. Filming crews were there all around us five or six days a week, sometimes twelve hours a day. It didn't make sense to meet with my sweet friends on camera. We had set up rules early on about being honest. The things we shared were personal. So the Muffins got put on hold. That was really hard for me, and I struggled with it. Then one day I was reminded of that verse in Ecclesiastes that says, "There is a time for everything, and a season for every activity under the heavens" (3:1). I had entered into a new season with *Duck Dynasty*. God had a plan for that too. My season of meeting with the Muffins was ending.

I was able to stay in touch with a lot of the Muffins, though. Many are still my friends to this day. I met Crystal, one of my best friends, in that group. The fruit of our times together as a group continues to grow.

From watching Miss Kay, I've learned a lot about what it means to nurture groups of women. She does that with me and with all the Robertsons, of course, but in her loving interaction with the Muffins and Celebrate Recovery at our church, I've seen her intentionality. I couldn't ask for a better teacher.

Have you ever led a mentoring group? I hope you're considering it now. This might be a challenge for you, especially if you're shy or introverted. That's okay. Take that first step toward being a part of something bigger than yourself. If you make sure to keep God at the center, you'll be blessed in ways you've never imagined.

Start by asking yourself, *What might I like to share?* If you love to bake, as Kay does, maybe it's muffins or another treat. Maybe you love to paint. In that case, invite friends over to paint. Love reading? Start a book group. Green thumb? Find some people to talk plants with. Too busy with family and work to start a group? Consider eating lunch with a friend once a week.

If you are feeling the tug to gather a group of women with the intention of finding true sisterhood, there are some important things to consider.

Scripture says that when two or more gather in the name of Jesus, he's right there.

Honesty. I've watched as women open up easily to Kay. You'd be surprised by the things they confide in her. Kay makes it easy by being honest about where she's been. She has experienced alcohol abuse, infidelity, and violence, and yet here she is, this incredible woman, admired and respected by so many. Women see that and think, *If she can do that, maybe I can find a way forward too.*

Flexibility. During the years that Kay met with the Muffins, I was always at work on Tuesday mornings, so I wasn't part of that group, though I would have loved to have been right there with Kay and those girls in the back of Darlene's dress shop. What I love is that it didn't matter a bit to Kay where they met. Around a picnic table or in the fellowship hall of a church building—it didn't matter. She cared about the people, not the place.

Have you ever started a conversation with someone in a line at the grocery store or Walmart or somewhere and felt the Spirit of the Lord right there in that ordinary place, guiding your conversation? Scripture says that when two or more gather in the name of Jesus, he's right there. So we can be very flexible about where we meet.

Fierce attitude. Remember the story of the woman who Kay followed home after she and her friend had words? Can't you just see Miss Kay throwing herself in the middle of that pair of young hotheads? I love that story, because it shows her ability to exhibit tough love. That's what love looks like, isn't it? It's not weak. It's bold. It's speaking the truth in love, heedless of getting a little scratched up in the process.

Conflicts flare up when we're part of a group, it's inevitable.

They might not be as dramatic as the one Miss Kay had to interrupt, but they will happen. What Miss Kay models for me is what professionals call a "non-anxious presence." She knows how to keep calm and stay focused on loving others well. When we do that, we can weather any conflict that might arise.

Consistency. Miss Kay knew her Muffins needed their weekly gathering as fuel—it gave them the hope and the energy they needed for the daily battles they faced. So she was consistent in meeting with them at a regularly scheduled time. Though she had plenty of other obligations, she prioritized the Muffins, and that shows great leadership and love, in my opinion.

Persistent prayer. The Muffins made prayer a priority. Every time they met, they'd pray together. They committed to pray for each other during the week too. And God honored those prayers.

I love how Kay's Muffins formed so organically and so naturally. God was really gracious to bring that group together. Sometimes joining an existing organized program makes more sense, depending on your season in life and your personality.

In the last few years, Kay and I have come alongside women in Celebrate Recovery, a Christ-centered 12-step program. I can't say enough about this program. It's designed for those struggling with addictions of any kind—food, love and relationships, alcohol and drugs, sex, gambling—as well as anger, codependency, and eating disorders. I especially appreciate how biblically based the program is, so I'm always learning

Show up and be present for the women in front of you. Actively choose to love them.

and growing alongside these women. And they like working with me, because I share how I've walked similar paths with so many of them.

I know God was preparing me for work with Celebrate Recovery. He did that through what I learned during not just the years Phil was walking on the dark side but also my time mentoring the Muffins, gathering with our monthly supper group, and filming *Duck Dynasty*. I sometimes wonder what he has planned for me next. Then I'll remember what Jesus said about how there's no need to worry about tomorrow (Matthew 6:34). There's plenty of work to be done and joy to be experienced in the season we're in right now. No need to rush.

However you choose to connect, remember what Phil always says: "Love God and love people." Love each other, flaws and all. We are called to do life together. With God at the center, you can't go wrong. Show up and be present for the women in front of you. Actively choose to love them. When you do, they'll recognize that you're for them and not against them.

I like to connect with people and show my love for them in my own unique way. I tend to think it looks a lot like a certain woman in the Bible named Lydia.

Lydia: Persistent in Purple (Acts 16)

> Now a certain woman named Lydia heard us. She was a seller of purple from the city of Thyatira, who worshiped God. The

Lord opened her heart to heed the things spoken by Paul. And when she and her household were baptized, she begged us, saying, "If you have judged me to be faithful to the Lord, come to my house and stay." So she persuaded us.

Now it happened, as we went to prayer, that a certain slave girl possessed with a spirit of divination met us, who brought her masters much profit by fortune-telling. This girl followed Paul and us, and cried out, saying, "These men are the servants of the Most High God, who proclaim to us the way of salvation." And this she did for many days.

But Paul, greatly annoyed, turned and said to the spirit, "I command you in the name of Jesus Christ to come out of her." And he came out that very hour. But when her masters saw that their hope of profit was gone, they seized Paul and Silas and dragged them into the marketplace to the authorities.

And they brought them to the magistrates, and said, "These men, being Jews, exceedingly trouble our city; and they teach customs which are not lawful for us, being Romans, to receive or observe." Then the multitude rose up together against them; and the magistrates tore off their clothes and commanded them to be beaten with rods. And when they had laid many stripes on them, they threw them into prison, commanding the jailer to keep them securely. Having received such a charge, he put them into the inner prison and fastened their feet in the stocks.

But at midnight Paul and Silas were praying and singing hymns to God, and the prisoners were listening to them. Suddenly there was a great earthquake, so that the foundations of the prison were shaken; and immediately all the

> doors were opened and everyone's chains were loosed. And the keeper of the prison, awaking from sleep and seeing the prison doors open, supposing the prisoners had fled, drew his sword and was about to kill himself. But Paul called with a loud voice, saying, "Do yourself no harm, for we are all here."
>
> Then he called for a light, ran in, and fell down trembling before Paul and Silas. And he brought them out and said, "Sirs, what must I do to be saved?"
>
> So they said, "Believe on the Lord Jesus Christ, and you will be saved, you and your household." Then they spoke the word of the Lord to him and to all who were in his house. And he took them the same hour of the night and washed their stripes. And immediately he and all his family were baptized. Now when he had brought them into his house, he set food before them; and he rejoiced, having believed in God with all his household. . . .
>
> So they went out of the prison and entered the house of Lydia; and when they had seen the brethren, they encouraged them and departed. (vv. 14–34, 40 NKJV)

I love the Bible, but sometimes it can be hard to relate to the female characters in Bible stories. Back then, women weren't afforded many rights at all. They had to be behind the scenes, and that's not me, really. But Lydia, seller of purple? I relate to her. Scripture tells us she was already a wealthy woman when she met Paul, Silas, and Timothy. In those days, only very wealthy people could afford purple fabric. Now, it's true that I was my family's little princess when I was growing up, but that's not why I relate to Lydia. There's way more to it than that.

Maybe you'll remember this story recounted in the book of Acts. Paul, Silas, and Timothy were traveling all over, preaching the good news. They were in the city of Philippi and went down to the river to pray. Lydia was there with some other women. They listened to Paul preach about Jesus. Scripture tells us Lydia was a worshiper of God. When she heard this good news about Jesus' life, death, burial, and resurrection, "the Lord opened her heart" and she responded to Paul's message (v. 14). Lydia asked Paul to baptize her, with all her household, and then she insisted that Paul, Silas, and Timothy be guests in her home during their stay in Philippi. Evidently they stayed there for some time.

Don't you love how Lydia showed such great hospitality? Some versions of the Bible say Lydia "persuaded" them. In other words, she wouldn't take no for an answer. I won't pretend to know what was going on in Lydia's mind, but it seems to me she cared for these men in response to the gift of salvation she'd just received through them from the Lord.

Scripture goes on to tell us that while Paul, Silas, and Timothy were in Philippi, a slave girl was following them, shouting, "These men are servants of the Most High God, who are telling you the way to be saved" (v. 17). She kept this up for days until finally Paul had enough. He commanded the spirit to come out of the girl, in the name of Jesus. This poor slave girl's prophecies had made her owners a lot of money. So they were mad about their loss of income. Can you imagine? They had Paul, Silas, and Timothy arrested, stripped, beaten, and thrown into prison for it. Even in that condition, the three continued to worship God, singing praises and praying. Then God sent an earthquake. The chains that bound them were broken and the prison doors were opened, but they stayed put. The prison guard was so astounded by their behavior that he, too, believed in Jesus. Paul baptized him and all his household.

Scripture tells us that afterward, Paul, Silas, and Timothy returned to Lydia's house, where they met with the brothers and sisters and "encouraged them" (v. 40). That group of believers at Lydia's house grew into what is now known as the church at Philippi—the folks Paul wrote the letter of Philippians to.

If you haven't read Philippians lately, I encourage you to read it. At the beginning of that letter, Paul called them his "partners in the gospel" and said, "I thank my God every time I remember you. In all my prayers for all of you, I always pray with joy because of your partnership in the gospel" (Philippians 1:3–5). You can tell Paul had a close relationship with the folks there—he called them partners. It's a very encouraging, short book full of joy.

Getting back to Lydia, there are three things I take away from her story.

First, hospitality is a natural reaction—a holy response—to God's goodness. When Lydia realized the guys who'd shared the gospel with her needed a place to stay, she knew what she needed to do. She had a home, so she shared it! It's like me feeding people. When I know somebody has a hungry belly, and I have a God-given gift for cooking, it makes sense that I share that gift. Maybe you're a singer or a painter or a networker or you love working with children. God wants you to share your gift. The world needs to hear your roar.

Hospitality is a natural reaction—a holy response—to God's goodness.

Shauna Niequist put it this way: "The heart of hospitality is about creating space for someone to feel seen and heard and loved. It's about declaring your table a safe zone, a place of warmth and nourishment."[9] We all have something others need. We don't have to offer that "space" in our homes. It can be anywhere. It's about responding to God's kindness by sharing what he gave us with others.

Second, sometimes, like Lydia, we need to insist on hospitality. Who knows what Paul, Silas, and Timothy were thinking when they tried to turn down Lydia. Maybe they thought they'd move on to the next city. Maybe they didn't want to impose. I don't know. All I know is that Lydia wouldn't take no for an answer. Remember how Lisa insists on giving Phyllis a hug every time she sees her? It might feel awkward at first, but showing our unconditional love is worth it. In Lydia's case, her insistence was key to that house church growing. There's no telling how many souls were saved! So insist on hospitality. Bake that extra lasagna and take it over. Slip that extra twenty into somebody's pocket. Write that encouraging note. Insist on hospitality. You are roaring, just in a different way.

Third, don't be prideful. If somebody is trying to bless you out of an abundance of love for the Lord, let them! Again, what if Paul hadn't accepted Lydia's invitation? There might not have been a church at Philippi. There might not be a book of Philippians. Don't deny someone the opportunity to love on you. You may have no idea what God is doing.

Hospitality is never wasted. It fulfills God's commands, it makes you feel good, and it helps others. I can't think of a better way to use your roar.

Your Turn

- Think about the most positive experience you've had with a group of women. What made that time special for you?
- How important is it to you that your confidants be honest? Flexible? Consistent?
- When and how do you pray for the women in your life? Is this an area where you'd like to grow?
- What gifts has God given you to share?
- In what ways do you feel most comfortable being hospitable? What areas are you not as comfortable?

7

Holy Math

Smaller Gatherings of Women

Where two or three gather in my name, there am I with them.

MATTHEW 18:20

Watching Miss Kay love on and nurture the Muffins inspired me. It showed me firsthand how Christian women can help one another through trials. Watching as one of my favorite sisters led a group of them was a marvel to me. I wished I could have participated, but at the time I was working a full-time job and raising two daughters. I had too much to do and too little time to get it all done. It was a different season for me. That was years ago. Now I'm in a new season, and I speak to women both in large groups and in one-on-ones.

Creating and leading a community of sisters may be the perfect next step for you in the season you're in. You could start your own Muffin group! It might be right in line with your gifting to reach out to other believing women to form such a gathering. If so, we want to encourage you. Decide on a time and place that works for you, then call up, text, or email a handful of women, and dive in!

On the other hand, maybe even baking a batch of muffins is more than you can manage, much less leading a group of women. If so, Kay and I totally relate. We have both been there. Family obligations, work schedules, health concerns—there are a host of good reasons why forming a group of sisters to meet may not make sense for you at the moment.

We want to extend an invitation to you, not create an obligation for you.

When you and I accepted Jesus, we were adopted into the

That's some kind of divine math, isn't it? One plus one equals three!

body of Christ. It's one of the many graces afforded us believers. As a member of the family of God, all we need is one other person to enjoy divine community. Check out what Jesus said to his disciples (that's us!):

> Again, truly I tell you that if two of you on earth agree about anything they ask for, it will be done for them by my Father in heaven. For where two or three gather in my name, there am I with them. (Matthew 18:19–20)

That's some kind of divine math, isn't it? One plus one equals three!

In this passage, Jesus was specifically referring to how we can pray together. It's also worth noticing that some special things happen when followers of Jesus get together.

Pretenses fall away when we're with other believers. We've all confessed our sinful nature and have a clean slate with God. We have nothing to hide, nothing to fear. This clean slate and gratitude for God's grace allows us to move quickly beyond the superficial to the spiritual.

We don't need to worry about comparisons, sizing up, and judgments that often happen among those who aren't "family." After all, as believers we intuitively know "all have sinned and fall short of the glory of God" (Romans 3:23). That makes us all aware that we're beneficiaries of God's grace when what we really deserve is God's wrath. In other words, nobody is uppity!

Jesus brings out the best in us. In the light of his unconditional love, we feel lighter, freer, more grateful. We're unafraid, bolder, braver, and more authentic, because we don't need to hide or feel shame—or try to be more than we really are. We become the best version of ourselves. And when we have Jesus, how can we not praise him? So our times together are filled with praise.

We encourage each other not to fret or worry. Instead of worrying, we pray, as Philippians 4:6–7 instructs.

> Let petitions and praises shape [our] worries into prayers, letting God know [our] concerns. Before you know it, a sense of God's wholeness, everything coming together for good, will come and settle you down. It's wonderful what happens when Christ displaces worry at the center of [our lives]. (THE MESSAGE)

So, whether you're gathered with one believer or two or more, Jesus is there, bringing out the best in you.

God invites us into conversation with him all the time and anytime (1 Thessalonians 5:17). He wants us to talk with him, to share what's going on. To unburden ourselves, so we can find rest in him (Matthew 11:28). We can ask anything of him (Matthew 21:22). He is faithful to supply all we need (Philippians 4:19). He is able to do anything, "more than all we ask or imagine" (Ephesians 3:20).

Most of all, we can be assured of his grace and peace because—back to that holy math—Jesus is right there with us.

Searching for Treasures of Scripture

One of my brothers-in-law, Jase, is big into treasure hunting. He takes his metal detector to places where there might be old coins or other historically significant items and hunts for hours—sometimes for days.

Exploring the Word of God is like that. There is rich treasure to be found within the pages of Scripture. Exploring with my sisters is one way to grow together, to find our communal roar. There is so much to explore—pretty much anything you could ever need. Verses in the book of Proverbs challenge us. When we're feeling down, the Psalms soothe us. And since the Gospels (Matthew, Mark, Luke, and John) tell Jesus' story from his close friends' point of view, spending time in those books feels like conversations with them. We find a wealth of wisdom, comfort, and knowledge there.

What is most exciting to me is how Scripture speaks to us differently, depending on where we are in life. According to Hebrews 4:12, Scripture is alive and active: "For the word of God is alive and active. Sharper than any double-edged sword, it penetrates even to dividing soul and spirit, joints and marrow; it judges the thoughts and attitudes of the heart."

Finally, there's so much hope to be found when we study God's Word together. "For everything that was written in the past was written to teach us, so that through the endurance taught in the Scriptures and the encouragement they provide *we might have hope*" (Romans 15:4, emphasis added).

Speaking the Truth

I've found it so important for sisters, when gathering together, to always speak the truth in love and not join in negative conversations, which is our bent as fallen humans. I was with some neighbors the other day when one friend started to complain about her husband. When she looked to me for agreement, I said, "Maybe you should give him a break." I explained that it didn't seem like he was intentionally trying to hurt her. He was trying his best. And he's just human. I reminded her of what the Bible says about not seeking after our own interests but the interests of others (Philippians 2:3–4). "Married couples sometimes have to be patient," I told her, "giving our spouses room to mess up, since we all do."

She seemed shocked by my words at first. Then she said, "Most of my friends pile on and say he needs to shape up or ship out. We all kind of bash our husbands, I guess."

I nodded to affirm what she was saying.

She continued to look thoughtful. "I don't know why I do that. Maybe I thought that since he annoyed me, I chose the wrong guy. So maybe it's not so much about him as it is about me," she admitted.

I thought that was pretty good. We often blame others for what we worry is wrong with us. That conversation reminded me of how we have to speak truth to one another. Seeing things from a different perspective can be just what we need to get in step with God's plan for our lives. It's like Scripture says: "Giving an honest answer is a sign of true friendship" (Proverbs 24:26 CEV).

Harmony of Purpose

When we gather together as believers, sisters enjoy the gift of harmony of purpose. We have a shared goal of giving glory to God.

When we gather together as believers, sisters enjoy the gift of harmony of purpose.

United in that shared purpose, a beautiful thing happens. God's love naturally manifests. It bubbles up and radiates out to everyone around us. Jesus spoke about his followers being like a "town built on a hill [that] cannot be hidden" (Matthew 5:14). United in pursuit of God's kingdom, his daughters give off a sort of glow.

Maybe you are like me and thinking about Miss Kay's Muffins has you excited about the idea of hosting. Or maybe not. Just the word *hospitality* is enough to make some women break out into a cold sweat. We have Martha Stewart to thank for taking hosting to a new, ridiculous level. She set impossible standards for those of us living ordinary lives. In fact, I think a lot of women decided they weren't the hosting kind simply because they saw the bar for what gathering friends together looked like, and they said, "Nah, that's not for me."

At some point, we even started using the word *entertaining* when it came to having people over or gathering friends. I don't think that word works for me. After all, if your guests need to be entertained, they're not really participating, are they?

Mary and the Gold Standard: Don't Miss Out

Let's go back to Scripture to look at the real gold standard of hospitality. We aim to gather with believing sisters to give glory to God, right? Martha Stewart didn't set this standard. We find it in Luke 10.

I want to keep Jesus at the center. I want to enjoy the presence of the Prince!

I don't want to get caught up in distractions. I want to keep Jesus at the center. I want to enjoy the presence of the Prince! Here are some ways to help minimize stress and maximize the glory of God when you're hosting your sisters.

- **Consider starting small.** Maybe you're one of those who like to go big or go home. But some of us tend to be better one-on-one. Being with a large group can be intimidating, so sometimes it's nice to do one-on-one for a while. As your comfort level grows, you can add people to the mix one at a time.
- **Keep it simple.** I love big, elaborate parties, but in all honesty, they can make me a little stressed. The expectations are often set too high. It's so much less pressure when things are casual. Gathering sisters shouldn't be about impressing anyone anyway, so limit the "many things" and focus on the important thing: Jesus.
- **Two-for-one.** Invite sisters to join you for something you've wanted to do. Go on a hike or a walk around the neighborhood. Sign up for a painting class. Clean out your garage together. If you want to make it more inviting, choose a treat like a manicure or a trip to the zoo.
- **Practice empathy.** Think about what might make it difficult for sisters to spend time with you, and then try to remove that barrier. For instance, if your friends have young children, the barrier might be childcare. Offer to meet at the park so the kids can play while you talk. If the barrier is limited time, meet her at her workplace for lunch or coffee and give her that much-needed break. If you

know a sister doesn't have transportation, offer to pick her up. It's all about being intentional and showing you care.

Your Turn

- What does your ideal gathering look like? One, two, three, more?
- Can you agree to meet regularly, whether that's weekly, monthly, or on some other schedule?
- What can you do to remove barriers that may be keeping women from joining your gathering?
- What would your agenda for your time together look like? Will you share a meal? Dig into a Bible study? Agreeing to a time and place up front will be helpful in managing expectations.
- Pray about who the Lord would have you meet with, and allow the Holy Spirit to guide your conversation. Be alert for opportunities to share God's Word.

8

What's Your Why?

Connections of the Heart

Declare his glory among the nations,
his marvelous deeds among all peoples.

PSALM 96:3

"After today, you'll be good as new. You'll never have to think about it again."

That's what the nurse said to me when, at the tender age of sixteen, I showed up at a clinic—pregnant, unmarried, and terrified. She said after they removed the "tissue" inside me, I could "move on" with my life. I nodded numbly. Her words echoed what my mom had said, so it had to be true, right? I allowed myself to swallow the lies and repeated the refrain, "I'll never have to think about this again."

Decades have passed, and I can assure you, every day I think about the child I allowed to be "removed" by an abortion doctor. Every. Single. Day. And let me tell you something else. Since going public about my abortion, I've spoken with too many women to count who say that the greatest regret of their lifetime is the same as mine: the choice to abort a baby.

Guilt and shame plagued me for years. I felt in my bones that what I had done was wrong. I told my husband, but otherwise I kept it hidden. It even cast a shadow over the joys of pregnancy and new motherhood. I hoped nobody would notice how it haunted me.

I told myself I'd made the decision when I was young. I had been in a tough spot, after all, and lacked guidance. What did I know? Still my secret tortured me. The shame grew and grew. I finally confessed it when I was facedown in the backyard. That's when Jesus met me in my brokenness and forgave me. He brought me into his loving light. Now I no longer live in shame, hiding my past. I've handed it over to Jesus to redeem—my past, my present, and my future. His redemption is still happening every single day.

Not everyone who has had an abortion reacts exactly as I did. Some respond with anger. They might even resent anyone who, like me, opposes the practice of abortion. This is often true of women who've been objectified, discarded, and expected to "handle" the situation on their own. For someone who has been controlled and dominated, the last thing they need is for a person to get up in their face and heap on more shame.

I don't offer shame. Many of us have had enough shame for a lifetime—more than enough. What I extend is what I've been given: the promise of redemption.

It was a choice, yes. It was the worst choice I ever made. However, because Christ died for me, I'm free from the guilt that once plagued me. I didn't "earn" this freedom. It was bought at a high price and given to me as a free, though costly, gift. Nobody can earn this gift. Jesus gives it not because we are good, but because *he* is good.

That's why I share my story. I want to see hearts changed and set free. It's what lights me up and makes me roar.

Afraid No More

To this day, talking about my abortion is difficult. It was one of the darkest days in my life—perhaps the darkest of all. I believe I will be reunited with my unborn child in heaven someday. I truly do. And I have no fear about what will happen if people learn about my "secret." I tell my story, believing that in God's hands it is being redeemed. My story can be of help to others. That's absolutely clear to me. I've seen evidence of that time and time again.

I want pregnant women to be assured of the love of God. Anyone blessed to have a life created within her has been shown favor by our God! The people around you may not be helpful, but there *are* people and organizations ready and waiting to serve women with unplanned pregnancies. Embrace Grace is one of our favorites, but there are many where dedicated, loving people serve daily with compassion. I tell the women I talk to that they can be supported and cared for. Do they have a choice to abort? Yes. But that choice comes with consequences far too heavy for any woman to bear. In the midst of a crisis, an "end" to the pregnancy can be appealing. But I personally know that aborting an unborn child is the most difficult and complicated choice. Choose life. Not just for your child, but for yourself!

There's another reason I share my story, and that's for those suffering under the weight and shame of having had an abortion. God has graciously helped me to heal spiritually and physically. I want them to see that healing is possible! We'll never forget, as the nurse falsely assured me, but we can experience joy again. As I share my story, I see women's eyes light up in hope when they see a way forward.

If you struggle with the aftereffects of trauma, as I did, please know that God loves you. If you let him, he will draw you close. He will enfold you in his loving arms. He will take away your burden and shame. He will set you free.

Choose life. Not just for your child, but for yourself!

As God continues to grant me opportunity, I will keep telling my story, trusting him with the rest.

I marvel at how God uses the worst day of my life in his redeeming work. It might seem strange that I could have been a pastor's wife for all those years and not been following Jesus. But I can tell you, it is absolutely possible. In my mind, I wasn't redeemable. I didn't feel worthy of the calling. I didn't feel I belonged in "the club." I didn't believe God could take away my sin. Once I came to the end of myself and he totally changed my life from the inside out, I was convinced of his power. It was as if I'd been blind and suddenly I could see. Now I see his power and presence all the time, and all I want to do is help people fall in love with Jesus.

Recently I got to speak to a large gathering of Christian believers and shared that an abortion is part of my story. Afterward a woman came up to talk with me. She'd been surprised by my confession and wanted to tell me something she'd never told anyone. Many years before she met her husband—who, like Al, was a pastor—she, too, had an abortion. She knew she'd been forgiven, but she had not told her husband or her grown children about it. *Why stir up the past?* she thought. But recently her church had begun a ministry specifically for women dealing with unplanned pregnancies, and she felt called to help. Still, she hadn't opened up to her family.

"I'm going home now to talk with them," she said. "It's time I stopped hiding what's already been forgiven. I believe

We have been given the light, sisters. We can't keep it to ourselves. We need to share it!

my story can help make a difference in the lives of those God has already gathered for me, right there in my home church."

Wow. Imagine how her decision will affect the lives of hurting and struggling women in her community! I felt in that moment that my own candle's flame was connecting with hers through God's providence, and that she was about to share that flame with many others. Maybe that's what Jesus meant when he said,

> Here's another way to put it: You're here to be light, bringing out the God-colors in the world. God is not a secret to be kept. We're going public with this, as public as a city on a hill. If I make you light-bearers, you don't think I'm going to hide you under a bucket, do you? I'm putting you on a light stand. Now that I've put you there on a hilltop, on a light stand—shine! Keep open house; be generous with your lives. By opening up to others, you'll prompt people to open up with God, this generous Father in heaven. (Matthew 5:14–16 THE MESSAGE)

We have been given the light, sisters. We can't keep it to ourselves. We need to share it!

Neighborhood Walks

As I've shared already in this book, I love the beach. Once our grown girls started having children of their own, we found ourselves wanting to share time with the grandkids by the ocean.

It was close enough to drive from home and invite friends and family, which we did often. It's a place where we have made many good memories. So we took the plunge. We found a place we liked and made it our own.

Since we were new to the community, in the evenings I'd walk with Al around our little neighborhood, meeting our neighbors. People could tell something was different about us, they said, and were curious about who we were, and we were glad to be making new friends. When word got out that Alan was a preacher, we received repeated requests to start a church. We're not always in Gulf Shores on Sundays, so we knew that wasn't a possibility. And besides, Alan preaches at White's Ferry Road Church in West Monroe, Louisiana, on a regular basis. In response to those requests, we'd say, "We're not starting a church, but how about you come to dinner?" That way we could talk and share the gospel in our home. Our neighborhood dinners led to providing counsel and service to many couples. It's also been a season spent developing some deep, lasting friendships.

One of these couples, Mike and Maleah, have become very special to us. When we decided to move from a condo and into a house nearby, they said, "If you're moving, we will too!" And they did! They bought a house next to ours. Maleah is really special, someone I greatly admire. I often say, "I want to be like you when I grow up, Maleah." As I've been candid with her about my story, not holding anything back, my vulnerability has opened a door. She shared some struggles too, and I've been able to share the gospel. The transformation in her is such a God-gift!

I've seen time and again how God steps into my

conversations with women, providing answers from his Word and help through the Holy Spirit. All I have to do is show up and love the woman in front of me. So that's what I try to do—invite them in and love on them. Maleah felt safe enough to share some deep struggles, and God somehow gave me words that helped, leading her to him.

It's funny, our reasons for moving made sense to us, but ultimately it didn't really matter. God has us here for *his* purpose. As we seek him, he keeps revealing that he has something bigger planned. That's pretty special!

It doesn't matter if you tell your story to a neighbor at the mailbox or declare it from a stage in a stadium. What matters is your willingness to do it. God will make a way. We cannot keep the news of God's goodness quiet. It's time to roar!

When Lisa shares her story, it's hard for me to remember the way she used to be. I hardly remember that haunted, troubled girl. I spend so much time with the redeemed Lisa that I struggle to recall how troubled she was before she gave her life over to the Lord. But that's the beauty of it! When she tells it, I just think, *God is so good!* The miracles God has done in my life and in Lisa's just couldn't have happened any other way. It makes me want to share the gospel all over again.

Have you ever thought about what would happen if we got as excited about saving folks from hell as we get about saving them from earthly troubles like COVID, cancer, and other things? I mean, think about it, we have the ultimate cure: the

All I have to do is show up and love the woman in front of me.

key to eternal life. The best news ever! Yet how often do we share the best news ever in the history of the world?

Sisters, it's really as simple as sharing our stories. It's not hard to do, and there's nothing to be ashamed of! The past is past, and the real work has already been done on the cross. All we have to do is tell how our lives have been changed by Jesus. He does the saving.

Ladies, think of it. We could be part of the greatest revival in history. It's like Lisa said about passing the flame. We could light this place up if we all share the gospel. It starts with one, and then that one tells the next. We just tell folks how Jesus was crucified, buried, and three days later resurrected, defeating death. And let them know that he's coming again in glory to judge the living and the dead—and to take believers to God's home to worship him forever.

Next thing you know, Jesus will come back and take us all to heaven. Then we'll hear those words we long to hear: "Well done, good and faithful servant!" (Matthew 25:21, 23).

I'm looking forward to that! There's such relief and joy that idea brings. Imagine being with God. Being assured that the journey is over. We're home.

I get excited when I think about enjoying heaven with the angels and all the followers of Christ. No matter what life throws at me, my first priority is seeing all my family in heaven—my husband, our daughters, their husbands, our grandchildren—the whole Robertson clan! I aim to take as many people along with me as possible. Nothing is more important.

A life redeemed, walking in faith, is a beautiful thing. Share it and the light multiplies. And the party in heaven will be beyond anything we could ever ask for or imagine!

I don't want anybody to have to live without Jesus—much less spend eternity without him. Spending even an hour, a moment, a second without the Lord was like hell for me. My life before salvation is a testimony to that. I can't imagine being separated from God for eternity. I'm willing to do whatever it takes to hold firm to the faith and be with him forever in heaven—and to take as many souls with me as I possibly can.

That's why *your* roar is so important. You can't keep it to yourself. A life redeemed, walking in faith, is a beautiful thing. Share it and the light multiplies. And the party in heaven will be beyond anything we could ever ask for or imagine!

Mary Magdalene: Survivor's Roar

> Now it came to pass, afterward, that He went through every city and village, preaching and bringing the glad tidings of the kingdom of God. And the twelve were with Him, and certain women who had been healed of evil spirits and infirmities—Mary called Magdalene, out of whom had come seven demons, and Joanna the wife of Chuza, Herod's steward, and Susanna, and many others who provided for Him from their substance. (Luke 8:1–3 NKJV)

Traumatic. That little word packs so much, doesn't it? We use it to describe those hurts, pains, births, deaths, injustices, and events that leave us hurt—be it emotionally or physically. After a trauma we are forever changed and altered.

Imagine how traumatic Jesus' crucifixion was for Mary

Magdalene. We know she was among those healed by Jesus (see above, Luke 8:1–3). Though she wasn't with him at the time he was seized in the garden of Gethsemane, she was present at his crucifixion. Witnessing that level of torture and death must have been beyond horrible. Imagine how helpless you'd feel if someone you love and admire were tortured, mocked, and humiliated literally to death. It would be perfectly reasonable to turn away or leave, but Mary stuck it out, watching as her Savior, so loving and full of power and goodness, gave himself up to die. It might even have been a relief to see him take that last breath. Hope must have felt so out of reach. She must have felt lonely too.

But Scripture tells us that Mary went home and observed the Sabbath day of rest, which would have included a meal and a prayer, and the next day she went with her friends to the tomb with spices and other supplies. This, to me, shows great love and devotion.

> The women who had come with Him from Galilee followed after, and they observed the tomb and how His body was laid. Then they returned and prepared spices and fragrant oils. And they rested on the Sabbath according to the commandment. (Luke 23:55–56 NKJV)

I have so much respect for Mary, who, unlike the disciples who locked themselves in a room in fear that they'd be arrested too, made her way to the place where her Savior was buried with plans to tenderly, carefully cleanse his mangled body and anoint it with myrrh and frankincense for burial. Remember those? Jesus' mother had been given these same spices by the kings who visited baby Jesus (see Matthew 2:11).

Arriving at the tomb, Mary and her friends met an angel. He told them the good news!

> Why do you seek the living among the dead? He is not here, but is risen! Remember how He spoke to you when He was still in Galilee, saying, "The Son of Man must be delivered into the hands of sinful men, and be crucified, and the third day rise again." (Luke 24:5–7 NKJV)

In my mind, after this, the women burst into a full-on sprint, rushing to the locked door of the room where the apostles were holed up!

Notice this, sister: the angel could have shown up in the locked room just as easily as the tomb. And yet, women were the first to hear the gospel! The angel implicitly told *them* to tell the others about their experience—to share the resurrection of Jesus. Forever after, the resurrection story would be shared in the context of Mary's unique story! Think about it. She would have said something like, "I was ready to prepare the body for burial because Jesus was so special to me, but I saw . . ."

Though God's power and glory is the focus here, this good news was received in light of Mary's specific witness. It mattered who gave this firsthand testimony because of her own history.

Sisters, we have to tell of God's glory in light of our own stories. That is how others will know and receive it as true.

Your Turn

- Take some time to reflect and be super honest about the hardest part of your life story. How has God redeemed it?
- Write about it—just for yourself and God.
- Ask the Lord to give you much compassion and boldness that you are willing to be vulnerable in sharing your story, so that others can come to know Christ.
- Pray for an opportunity to share your story, and then be sensitive to the Holy Spirit's promptings. He's likely to surprise you with opportunities you never could have dreamed up!
- What might revival look like if just half of your neighbors came to salvation through your roar?

9

Our Forever Home

With the Lion and the Lamb

Do not weep! See, the Lion of the tribe of Judah, the Root of David, has triumphed.

REVELATION 5:5

Sisters, our job isn't to save the world. It's to point people to the One who saves!

Whether you raise your roar to the glory of God today in your home or your workplace or on the street, you are not alone. I love how Scripture says we are surrounded by a "great cloud of witnesses" (Hebrews 12:1). That unity in the body of Christ gives us great assurance! Besides, in faith we know, at the end of time, all of us sisters will be together in heaven! The very best moments of our lives on earth cannot compare with the joy we will experience there. I think of how full my heart was at the birth of my grandchildren and on my wedding day. But those days will pale in comparison. Can you even imagine?

What's funny is that everybody's got a different idea of what heaven will be like. Sometimes I think it's like the garden Nanny grew. She grew vegetables and fruit trees, but my favorite part was her beautiful flower garden with a path you could meander through. She had a row of sweet-smelling gardenias and a wisteria tree that wound up around a trellis with bundles of trailing purple flowers. On one side of the path were early bloom zinnias with their cheery hues of pink, yellow, and purple, along with perky yellow daffodils and elegant white narcissus with their strong, musky scent. On the other side of the path were world-class rosebushes of all kinds and colors. Nanny

Sisters, our job isn't to save the world. It's to point people to the One who saves!

gathered whatever was in bloom to make bouquets for the Sunday church services. It was her way of offering back to the Lord what he'd created.

Nanny's gardens were blissful to me. The smells, the gorgeous colors and textures, the loving care that went into every bloom and bouquet. But can you imagine the gardens God has in heaven? Take a look at what John saw when he got a glimpse of heaven:

> Then the angel showed me the river of the water of life, as clear as crystal, flowing from the throne of God and of the Lamb down the middle of the great street of the city. On each side of the river stood the tree of life, bearing twelve crops of fruit, yielding its fruit every month. And the leaves of the tree are for the healing of the nations. No longer will there be any curse. The throne of God and of the Lamb will be in the city, and his servants will serve him. They will see his face, and his name will be on their foreheads. There will be no more night. They will not need the light of a lamp or the light of the sun, for the Lord God will give them light. And they will reign for ever and ever. (Revelation 22:1–5)

I hope heaven has a beach. And Al would probably like a place to play golf. In John's vision, he saw a river, which I know my father-in-law and a bunch of the men in our family would enjoy, because that way there'd be fishing and duck hunting in heaven.

But when I think of heaven, I often think of the song "I Can Only Imagine," because, like Bart Millard, the author of that song, I'm ready to go there but my mind simply can't comprehend how wonderful it will be! I do know that in heaven we'll live in eternity with God, where there will be no tears, no sorrow, no darkness. We'll have let go of our worn-out bodies. Scripture says that Jesus will transform our earthly bodies into glorious ones like his, beautiful and whole (Philippians 3:20–21).

I long for the day when I receive that inheritance! It's like the greatest gift of all—a gift waiting to be unwrapped at the end of our days. The Bible says God has our inheritance stored up for us in heaven, where it will never decay or be ruined or disappear (1 Peter 1:3–9). Best of all, I'll be with him, praising him and enjoying him.

I love my family and my home, but God promises that my heavenly home will be even better. So many people I love are already there, including my father, whom I loved so much. Each year when his birthday comes around and on every Father's Day and Christmas Day and on any special day we celebrate, I imagine him in heaven with his father. My mother is there. My sister is there. My brother is there. My grandparents. My baby, of course. And many dear friends.

I'd want to go even if they weren't there, but thinking of reuniting with loved ones makes it even sweeter. When a friend or family member dies, I think, *They're in heaven! They're in an incredible place in the presence of the Father and my brother Jesus.* Imagine! Imagine praising God there and just being amazed at what heaven is.

Who knows, I might dance—or fall down on my knees!

How will I get there? Jesus promised to come back and take those who believe in him to heaven. We have his word on that:

> Don't be worried! Have faith in God and have faith in me. There are many rooms in my Father's house. I wouldn't tell you this, unless it was true. I am going there to prepare a place for each of you. After I have done this, I will come back and take you with me. Then we will be together. (John 14:1–3 CEV)

And if I die before the Lord returns, I'll go straight to heaven, for Scripture tells us "to be absent from the body [is] to be present with the Lord" (2 Corinthians 5:8 NKJV).

I have a friend who was raised on a farm in Oklahoma. One day on the farm, her precious mother, an angel to all who knew her, was struck by lightning. It fatally burned the insides of her body, so the best they could do was keep her comfortable. She was a faith-filled Christian woman. In the hospital, before she drew her last breath, she looked at her husband. He told her he loved her, and she told him that she loved him. Then she said, "I'm ready to go home to my Lord." And she closed her eyes, smiled, and was gone.

She had eagerly awaited the coming of her Lord. Her family believes that as she smiled and drew her last breath, she met him. In an instant, the Lord met her, and she's now in his presence forever. How could I ever wish for more than that?

Like the song says, I can only imagine.

That's why we pray that you, sister, will find your voice and use it for the glory of God! Tap into the blessing of community and be persistent in hospitality. When women of faith cheer each other on, it's so, so good! I don't know about you, but I think all that love and goodness sounds like heaven on earth.

Your Turn

- When you imagine heaven, what comes to mind?
- Who are you looking forward to being with in heaven?
- What do you most look forward to doing in heaven?
- Whose roar can you point to as helping you get through life and to heaven someday?
- What steps can you take to lay up the treasure of friends and family in heaven?

Acknowledgments

We would like to thank Ami for being our writer and for "reading us" effectively.

Thank you, Sealy, for being with us and being our cheerleader throughout the entire process.

We would like to thank Nelson Books for their trust in us to come up with a book to bless others and, most importantly, our heavenly Father. Without his grace, love, and forgiveness, we would not be the women, sisters, mothers, grandmothers or great-grandmothers he made us to be. We are eternally thankful to him.

Scripture

Introduction: Hello, Sister!

I pray that the eyes of your heart may be enlightened in order that you may know the hope to which he has called you, the riches of his glorious inheritance in his holy people.

EPHESIANS 1:18

You are God's chosen and special people. You are a group of royal priests and a holy nation. God has brought you out of darkness into his marvelous light. Now you must tell all the wonderful things that he has done. The Scriptures say,

> "Once you were nobody.
>   Now you are God's people.
> At one time no one
>   had pity on you.
> Now God has treated you
>   with kindness."

1 PETER 2:9–10 CEV

See, the Lion of the tribe of Judah, the Root of David, has triumphed. He is able to open the scroll and its seven seals.

REVELATION 5:5

You made all the delicate, inner parts of my body
and knit me together in my mother's womb.
Thank you for making me so wonderfully complex!
Your workmanship is marvelous—how well I know it.

PSALM 139:13–14 NLT

The LORD keeps watch over you as you come and go,
both now and forever.

PSALM 121:8 NLT

For we are his workmanship, created in Christ Jesus for good works, which God prepared beforehand, that we should walk in them.

EPHESIANS 2:10 ESV

The Spirit of the LORD is upon Me,
Because He has anointed Me
To preach the gospel to the poor;
He has sent Me to heal the brokenhearted,
To proclaim liberty to the captives
And recovery of sight to the blind,
To set at liberty those who are oppressed;
To proclaim the acceptable year of the LORD.

LUKE 4:18–19 NKJV

In the world you will have tribulation; but be of good cheer, I have overcome the world.

JOHN 16:33 NKJV

Chapter 1: Made to Roar

Tell every nation on earth,
"The LORD is wonderful
and does marvelous things!"

1 CHRONICLES 16:24 CEV

[God] knit me together in my mother's womb.

PSALM 139:13

We are God's masterpiece. He has created us anew in Christ Jesus, so we can do the good things he planned for us long ago.

EPHESIANS 2:10 NLT

Suffering produces perseverance; perseverance, character; and character, hope. And hope does not put us to shame, because God's love has been poured out into our hearts through the Holy Spirit, who has been given to us.

ROMANS 5:3–5

The thief does not come except to steal, and to kill, and to destroy. I have come that they may have life, and that they may have it more abundantly.

JOHN 10:10 NKJV

We know that in all things God works for the good of those who love him, who have been called according to his purpose.

ROMANS 8:28

Everything in the Scriptures is God's Word. All of it is useful for teaching and helping people and for correcting them and showing them how to live.

2 TIMOTHY 3:16 CEV

Now a woman, having a flow of blood for twelve years, who had spent all her livelihood on physicians and could not be healed by any, came from behind and touched the border of His garment. And immediately her flow of blood stopped.

And Jesus said, "Who touched Me?"

When all denied it, Peter and those with him said, "Master, the multitudes throng and press You, and You say, 'Who touched Me?'"

But Jesus said, "Somebody touched Me, for I perceived power going out from Me."

Now when the woman saw that she was not hidden, she came trembling; and falling down before Him, she declared to Him in the presence of all the people the reason she had touched Him and how she was healed immediately.

And He said to her, "Daughter, be of good cheer; your faith has made you well. Go in peace."

LUKE 8:43–48 NKJV

Chapter 2: Hungry, Hungry, Hungry

The righteous eats to the satisfying of his soul,
But the stomach of the wicked shall be in want.

PROVERBS 13:25 NKJV

Hope deferred makes the heart sick,
But when the desire comes, it is a tree of life.

PROVERBS 13:12 NKJV

My soul thirsts for God, for the living God.
When shall I come and appear before God?

PSALM 42:2 NKJV

He satisfies the longing soul,
and the *hungry soul* he fills with good things.

PSALM 107:9 ESV, EMPHASIS ADDED

I am the bread of life; whoever comes to me shall not hunger, and whoever believes in me shall never thirst.

JOHN 6:35 ESV

Now Jesus learned that the Pharisees had heard that he was gaining and baptizing more disciples than John—although in fact it was not Jesus who baptized, but his disciples. So he left Judea and went back once more to Galilee.

Now he had to go through Samaria. So he came to a town in Samaria called Sychar, near the plot of ground Jacob had given to his son Joseph. Jacob's well was there, and Jesus, tired as he was from the journey, sat down by the well. It was about noon.

JOHN 4:1–6

"You are a Jew and I am a Samaritan woman. How can you ask me for a drink?" (For Jews do not associate with Samaritans.)

Jesus answered her, "If you knew the gift of God and who it is that asks you for a drink, you would have asked him and he would have given you living water."

"Sir," the woman said, "you have nothing to draw with and the well is deep. Where can you get this living water? Are you greater than our father Jacob, who gave us the well and drank from it himself, as did also his sons and his livestock?"

Jesus answered, "Everyone who drinks this water will be thirsty again, but whoever drinks the water I give them will never thirst. Indeed, the water I give them will become in them a spring of water welling up to eternal life."

The woman said to him, "Sir, give me this water so that I won't get thirsty and have to keep coming here to draw water."

He told her, "Go, call your husband and come back."

"I have no husband," she replied.

Jesus said to her, "You are right when you say you have no husband. The fact is, you have had five husbands, and the man you now have is not your husband."

JOHN 4:9–18

"A time is coming and has now come when the true worshipers will worship the Father in the Spirit and in truth, for they are the kind of worshipers the Father seeks. God is spirit, and his worshipers must worship in the Spirit and *in truth.*"

The woman said, "I know that Messiah" (called Christ) "is coming. When he comes, he will explain everything to us."

Then Jesus declared, "I, the one speaking to you—I am he."

JOHN 4:23–26, EMPHASIS ADDED

Many of the Samaritans from that town believed in him because of the woman's testimony, "He told me everything I ever did." So when the Samaritans came to him, they urged him to stay with them, and he stayed two days. And because of his words many more became believers. They said to the woman, "We no longer believe just because of what you said; now we have heard for ourselves, and we know that this man really is the Savior of the world."

JOHN 4:39–42

The Spirit and the bride say, "Come!"
Everyone who hears this should say, "Come!"
If you are thirsty, come! If you want life-giving
water, come and take it! It's free!

REVELATION 22:17 CEV

Every good and perfect gift is from above, coming down from the Father of the heavenly lights, who does not change like shifting shadows.

JAMES 1:17

Here on earth you *will* have many trials and sorrows.

JOHN 16:33 NLT, EMPHASIS ADDED

As the One who called you is holy, you also are to be holy in all your conduct; for it is written, Be holy, because I am holy.

1 PETER 1:15–16 HCSB

God blesses those people
who want to obey him
more than to eat or drink.
They will be given
what they want!

MATTHEW 5:6 CEV

Chapter 3: Welcome to the Pride

The Lord directs the steps of the godly.
He delights in every detail of their lives.

PSALM 37:23 NLT

For if you remain silent at this time, relief and deliverance for the Jews will arise from another place, but you and your father's family will perish. And who knows but that you have come to your royal position for such a time as this?

ESTHER 4:14

Chapter 4: Look Who's Talking

Those who look to him are radiant;
their faces are never covered with shame.

PSALM 34:5

[Contemplating] the Lord's glory, [we] are being *transformed* into his image with ever-increasing glory, which comes from the Lord, who is the Spirit.

2 CORINTHIANS 3:18, EMPHASIS ADDED

As a deer longs for streams of water,
so I long for You, God.
I thirst for God, the living God.

PSALM 42:1–2 HCSB

Sing to the LORD a new song;
sing to the LORD, all the earth.

PSALM 96:1

Confess your sins to each other.

JAMES 5:16

Be alert and of sober mind. Your enemy the devil prowls around like a roaring lion looking for someone to devour.

1 PETER 5:8

For though we live in the body, we do not wage war in an unspiritual way, since the weapons of our warfare are not worldly, but are powerful through God for the demolition of strongholds. We demolish arguments and every high-minded thing that is raised up against the knowledge of God, taking every thought captive to obey Christ.

2 CORINTHIANS 10:3–5 HCSB

Do not be afraid, for I have ransomed you.
I have called you by name; you are mine.
When you go through deep waters,
I will be with you.
When you go through rivers of difficulty,
you will not drown.

When you walk through the fire of oppression,
you will not be burned up;
the flames will not consume you.

ISAIAH 43:1–2 NLT

For God has not given us a spirit of fear and timidity, but of power, love, and self-discipline.

2 TIMOTHY 1:7 NLT

Let your conduct be without covetousness; be content with such things as you have. For He Himself has said, "I will never leave you nor forsake you." So we may boldly say:

"The LORD is my helper;
I will not fear.
What can man do to me?"

HEBREWS 13:5–6 NKJV

But when [Jochebed] could no longer hide him, she took an ark of bulrushes for him, daubed it with asphalt and pitch, put the child in it, and laid it in the reeds by the river's bank. And his sister stood afar off, to know what would be done to him.

Then the daughter of Pharaoh came down to bathe at the river. And her maidens walked along the riverside; and when she saw the ark among the reeds, she sent her maid to get it. And when she opened it, she saw the child, and behold, the baby wept. So she had compassion on him, and said, "This is one of the Hebrews' children."

Then his sister said to Pharaoh's daughter, "Shall I go and call a nurse for you from the Hebrew women, that she may nurse the child for you?"

EXODUS 2:3–7 NKJV

Now it came to pass in those days, when Moses was grown, that he went out to his brethren and looked at their burdens. And he saw an Egyptian beating a Hebrew, one of his brethren. So he looked this way and that way, and when he saw no one, he killed the Egyptian and hid him in the sand. And when he went out the second day, behold, two Hebrew men were fighting, and he said to the one who did the wrong, "Why are you striking your companion?"

Then he said, "Who made you a prince and a judge over us? Do you intend to kill me as you killed the Egyptian?"

So Moses feared and said, "Surely this thing is known!" When Pharaoh heard of this matter, he sought to kill Moses. But Moses fled from the face of Pharaoh and dwelt in the land of Midian; and he sat down by a well.

EXODUS 2:11–15 NKJV

For the horses of Pharaoh went with his chariots and his horsemen into the sea, and the LORD brought back the waters of the sea upon them. But the children of Israel went on dry land in the midst of the sea.

Then Miriam the prophetess, the sister of Aaron, took the timbrel in her hand; and all the women went out after her with timbrels and with dances. And Miriam answered them:

"Sing to the LORD,
For He has triumphed gloriously!

> The Lord and his disciples were traveling along and came to a village. When they got there, a woman named Martha welcomed him into her home. She had a sister named Mary, who sat down in front of the Lord and was listening to what he said. Martha was worried about all that had to be done. Finally, she went to Jesus and said, "Lord, doesn't it bother you that my sister has left me to do all the work by myself? Tell her to come and help me!" (vv. 38–40 CEV)

I can't help but laugh at this. Martha boldly invited Jesus into her home, and now here she's bold again, basically demanding that he take her side in an argument!

> The Lord answered, "Martha, Martha! You are worried and upset about so many things, but only one thing is necessary. Mary has chosen what is best, and it will not be taken away from her." (vv. 41–42 CEV)

I feel a little bad for Martha, don't you? She was the one who invited Jesus over, but Mary was the one getting to enjoy his company. I can understand why Martha got upset. Her complaint that her sister was not helping with the housekeeping and food preparation makes sense to me. But what did Jesus say? He pointed out that even though she invited him in, she was not enjoying his presence, because she was not living in the moment.

Whoa. That's good. She had Jesus right there, and yet she was so caught up in the trappings of housekeeping and being a good hostess that she got stressed—and almost missed out on the presence of the Prince of Peace!

The horse and its rider
He has thrown into the sea!"

EXODUS 15:19–21 NKJV

Chapter 5: The Power of Connection

Be good friends who love deeply.

ROMANS 12:10 THE MESSAGE

Confess your sins to each other and pray for each other so that you may be healed.

JAMES 5:16

God's very own . . . [who] can show others the goodness of God, for he called you out of the darkness into his wonderful light.

1 PETER 2:9 NLT

By this everyone will know that you are my disciples, if you love one another.

JOHN 13:35

Chapter 6: Kay's Muffins

Let us consider how we may spur one another on toward love and good deeds, not giving up meeting together . . . but encouraging one another—and all the more as you see the Day approaching.

HEBREWS 10:24–25

> See, I am doing a new thing!
> Now it springs up; do you not perceive it?

ISAIAH 43:19

Guide older women into lives of reverence so they end up as neither gossips nor drunks, but models of goodness. By looking at them, the younger women will know how to love their husbands and children, be virtuous and pure, keep a good house, be good wives.

TITUS 2:3–5 THE MESSAGE

> There is a time for everything,
> and a season for every activity under the heavens.

ECCLESIASTES 3:1

Now a certain woman named Lydia heard us. She was a seller of purple from the city of Thyatira, who worshiped God. The Lord opened her heart to heed the things spoken by Paul. And when she and her household were baptized, she begged us, saying, "If you have judged me to be faithful to the Lord, come to my house and stay." So she persuaded us.

Now it happened, as we went to prayer, that a certain slave girl possessed with a spirit of divination met us, who brought her masters much profit by fortune-telling. This girl followed Paul and us, and cried out, saying, "These men are the servants of the Most High God, who proclaim to us the way of salvation." And this she did for many days.

But Paul, greatly annoyed, turned and said to the spirit, "I command you in the name of Jesus Christ to come out of her." And he came out that very hour. But when her masters saw that their hope of profit was gone, they seized Paul and Silas and dragged them into the marketplace to the authorities.

And they brought them to the magistrates, and said, "These men, being Jews, exceedingly trouble our city; and they teach customs which are not lawful for us, being Romans, to receive or observe." Then the multitude rose up together against them; and the magistrates tore off their clothes and commanded them to be beaten with rods. And when they had laid many stripes on them, they threw them into prison, commanding the jailer to keep them securely. Having received such a charge, he put them into the inner prison and fastened their feet in the stocks.

But at midnight Paul and Silas were praying and singing hymns to God, and the prisoners were listening to them. Suddenly there was a great earthquake, so that the foundations of the prison were shaken; and immediately all the doors were opened and everyone's chains were loosed. And the keeper of the prison, awaking from sleep and seeing the prison doors open, supposing the prisoners had fled, drew his sword and was about to kill himself. But Paul called with a loud voice, saying, "Do yourself no harm, for we are all here."

Then he called for a light, ran in, and fell down trembling before Paul and Silas. And he brought them out and said, "Sirs, what must I do to be saved?"

So they said, "Believe on the Lord Jesus Christ, and you will be saved, you and your household." Then they spoke the word of the Lord to him and to all who were in his house. And he took them the same hour of the night and washed their stripes. And immediately he and all his family were baptized. Now when he had brought them into his house, he set food before them; and he rejoiced, having believed in God with all his household. . . .

So they went out of the prison and entered the house of Lydia; and when they had seen the brethren, they encouraged them and departed.

ACTS 16:14–34, 40 NKJV

I thank my God every time I remember you. In all my prayers for all of you, I always pray with joy because of your partnership in the gospel.

PHILIPPIANS 1:3–5

Chapter 7: Holy Math

Again, truly I tell you that if two of you on earth agree about anything they ask for, it will be done for them by my Father in heaven. For where two or three gather in my name, there am I with them.

MATTHEW 18:19–20

All have sinned and fall short of the glory of God.

ROMANS 3:23

Let petitions and praises shape [our] worries into prayers, letting God know [our] concerns. Before you know it, a sense of God's wholeness, everything coming together for good, will come and settle you down. It's wonderful what happens when Christ displaces worry at the center of your life.

PHILIPPIANS 4:6–7 THE MESSAGE

Now to him who is able to do immeasurably more than all we ask or imagine, according to his power that is at work within us.

EPHESIANS 3:20

For the word of God is alive and active. Sharper than any double-edged sword, it penetrates even to dividing soul and spirit, joints and marrow; it judges the thoughts and attitudes of the heart.

HEBREWS 4:12

For everything that was written in the past was written to teach us, so that through the endurance taught in the Scriptures and the encouragement they provide *we might have hope.*

ROMANS 15:4, EMPHASIS ADDED

Giving an honest answer
is a sign
of true friendship.

PROVERBS 24:26 CEV

You are the light of the world. A town built on a hill [that] cannot be hidden.

MATTHEW 5:14

The Lord and his disciples were traveling along and came to a village. When they got there, a woman named Martha welcomed him into her home. She had a sister named Mary, who sat down in front of the Lord and was listening to what he said. Martha was worried about all that had to be done. Finally, she went to Jesus and said, "Lord, doesn't it bother you that my sister has left me to do all the work by myself? Tell her to come help me!"

The Lord answered, "Martha, Martha! You are worried and upset about so many things, but only one thing is necessary. Mary has chosen what is best, and it will not be taken away from her."

LUKE 10:38–42 CEV

Chapter 8: What's Your Why?

Declare his glory among the nations,
his marvelous deeds among all peoples.

PSALM 96:3

Here's another way to put it: You're here to be light, bringing out the God-colors in the world. God is not a secret to be kept. We're going public with this, as public as a city on a hill. If I make you light-bearers, you don't think I'm going to hide you under a bucket, do you? I'm putting you on a light stand. Now that I've put you there on a hilltop, on a light stand—shine! Keep open house; be generous with your lives. By opening up to others, you'll prompt people to open up with God, this generous Father in heaven.

MATTHEW 5:14–16 THE MESSAGE

Well done, good and faithful servant!

MATTHEW 25:21, 23

Now it came to pass, afterward, that He went through every city and village, preaching and bringing the glad tidings of the kingdom of God. And the twelve were with Him, and certain women who had been healed of evil spirits and infirmities—Mary called

Magdalene, out of whom had come seven demons, and Joanna the wife of Chuza, Herod's steward, and Susanna, and many others who provided for Him from their substance.

LUKE 8:1–3 NKJV

The women who had come with Him from Galilee followed after, and they observed the tomb and how His body was laid. Then they returned and prepared spices and fragrant oils. And they rested on the Sabbath according to the commandment.

LUKE 23:55–56 NKJV

Why do you seek the living among the dead? He is not here, but is risen! Remember how He spoke to you when He was still in Galilee, saying, "The Son of Man must be delivered into the hands of sinful men, and be crucified, and the third day rise again."

LUKE 24:5–7 NKJV

Chapter 9: Our Forever Home

Do not weep! See, the Lion of the tribe of Judah, the Root of David, has triumphed.

REVELATION 5:5

Therefore, since we are surrounded by such a great cloud of witnesses, let us throw off everything that hinders and the sin that so easily entangles.

HEBREWS 12:1

Then the angel showed me the river of the water of life, as clear as crystal, flowing from the throne of God and of the Lamb down the middle of the great street of the city. On each side of the river stood the tree of life, bearing twelve crops of fruit, yielding its fruit every month. And the leaves of the tree are for the healing of the nations. No longer will there be any curse. The throne of God and of the Lamb will be in the city, and his servants will serve him. They will see his face, and his name will be on their foreheads. There will be no more night. They will not need the light of a lamp or the light of the sun, for the Lord God will give them light. And they will reign for ever and ever.

REVELATION 22:1–5

Don't be worried! Have faith in God and have faith in me. There are many rooms in my Father's house. I wouldn't tell you this, unless it was true. I am going there to prepare a place for each of you. After I have done this, I will come back and take you with me. Then we will be together.

JOHN 14:1–3 CEV

We are confident, yes, well pleased rather to be absent from the body [is] to be present with the Lord.

2 CORINTHIANS 5:8 NKJV

Notes

1. A lion or tiger can roar as loud as 114 decibels. Sarah Zielinski, "Secrets of a Lion's Roar," *Smithsonian Magazine*, November 3, 2011, https://www.smithsonianmag.com/science-nature/secrets-of-a-lions-roar-126395997/.
2. Kerry McDonald, "Harvard Study: An Epidemic of Loneliness Is Spreading Across America," Foundation for Economic Education, February 19, 2021, https://fee.org/articles/harvard-study-an-epidemic-of-loneliness-is-spreading-across-america/. See also Vivek Murthy, "Work and Loneliness Epidemic," *Harvard Business Review*, September 16, 2017, https://hbr.org/2017/09/work-and-the-loneliness-epidemic.
3. Joni Eareckson Tada, *Finding God in Hidden Places: His Presence in the Pieces of Our Lives* (Eugene, OR: Harvest House, 2010), 84.
4. Kim Parker et al., "Demographic and Economic Trends in Urban, Suburban and Rural Communities," in *What Unites and Divides Urban, Suburban and Rural Communities*, Pew Research Center, May 22, 2018, https://www.pewresearch.org/social-trends/2018/05/22/demographic-and-economic-trends-in-urban-suburban-and-rural-communities/.
5. "Divorce Rate by State 2021," World Population Review, accessed October 13, 2021, https://worldpopulationreview.com/state-rankings/divorce-rate-by-state.
6. "82% of Young Adults Say Society Is in a Leadership Crisis," Barna, October 30, 2019, https://www.barna.com/research/leadership-crisis/.

7. George A. Akerlof and Janet L. Yellen, "An Analysis of Out-of-Wedlock Births in the United States," Brookings, August 1, 1996, https://www.brookings.edu/research/an-analysis-of-out-of-wedlock-births-in-the-united-states/.
8. Jeffrey M. Jones, "U.S. Church Membership Falls Below Majority for First Time," Gallup, March 29, 2021, https://news.gallup.com/poll/341963/church-membership-falls-below-majority-first-time.aspx.
9. Shauna Niequist, *Bread and Wine: A Love Letter to Life Around the Table with Recipes* (Grand Rapids: Zondervan, 2013), 126.

About the Authors

Miss Kay Robertson is the Robertson family matriarch—wife of Phil and the backbone and funny bone of the family. You may have seen her on television, eaten at her restaurant, or drooled your way through one of her *New York Times* bestselling cookbooks.

Lisa Robertson is her daughter-in-law, married to Alan, who is often referred to as the "beardless brother," though, truth be told, he sports a short one these days. The Robertson family lives in West Monroe, Louisiana.